By Guo, Li

**Canada International Press**

Title: A Flying Dad

Author: Guo, Li (Text dictated, proofread)

Compiled: by Guo, Li's friends

Photographer: Jianting Guo, Hong Xin, Tina Y. Zhang,
Sally Zhu, etc.

Publisher: Canada International Press

www.intlpressca.com Email: service@intlpressca.com

First Edition in Canada: Dec. 2024

First Printing: Dec. 2024

Printed Edition ISBN: 978-1-998479-24-5

E-Book ISBN: 978-1-998479-25-2

# Introduction

Guo, Li (郭利 in Chinese), this name has become a symbol in China's melamine-tainted infant formula incident, an ordinary man who works tirelessly for real justice and truth. His story is not only the personal experience of a Beijing father fighting for his child's health, but also a profound interrogation of social justice and the rule of law in China as a whole.

In 2008, China shocked the world with the melamine-tainted infant formula scandal. Hundreds of thousands of infants and young children, including Guo's own child, have suffered from urinary system diseases after consuming milk powder containing deadly chemicals. In this new stage of life that should be full of hope and happiness, many Chinese families have fallen into endless pain and despair. However, in the face of this tragedy, different people chose different paths of struggle. Some were silent, some compromised, but Guo chose to fight and defend.

As an ordinary consumer and parent of a victim, Guo originally just wanted fairness and hoped to seek justice for his child through legal means. However, what he faced was not only the dairy corporate irresponsibility, but also various injustices in the Chinese judiciary system. China Mengniu Yashily Int'l Group framed him for extortion and he was sentenced to five years in prison. During this time, he lost his freedom, but not his faith. His body was imprisoned, but his spirit remained strong.

After being released from a Jieyang prison, Guo used all legal means to appeal and was eventually found not guilty by the Guangdong Provincial High Court. However, when he applied for his state compensations, he was rejected again. This series of twists & turns allows us to catch sight of many obstacles faced by a middle-class man in the pursuit of fairness and justice, as well as the huge psychological pressure and life difficulties caused by Chinese institutional oppression.

Now, Guo has recorded every detail of his rights defending process over the years in a book. This is a true brave and total disclosure, a comprehensive reflection on his own experience, and a serious criticism of Chinese current social situation. He told us from his suffering experience: even in the darkest times, never give up hope, even in the face of evil forces (雅势力) or the powerful enemies, people must stick to the truth, even if you are alone and helpless, you must believe that justice will eventually come.

Guo Li's new book is not only a history of his personal human rights struggle, but also a live witness to the times. It reminds us that every individual may become a tiny speck of dust in the torrent of history, but every small voice gathered together can form a great tide that changes the world.

I hope readers from all over the world will feel that persistence and determination of Guo, cherish our existing legal environment, jointly promote our social progress, so that more men like Guo will no longer be alone and helpless in the pursuit of fairness and justice in and outside China.

With this INTRO., I pay tribute to those who continue to fight firmly for truth, fairness, and justice!

QIAO Long (乔龙)
Senior News Reporter in Chinese,
The Mainstream American Media
September 28th, 2024 HK

# Author's Remarks

In the class at a famous institution of higher learning, a student answered the professor's question: "Evil does not exist, Professor, to speak the least, Evil itself does not exist. There is evilness only because there is no God in your heart, just like darkness and cold.  Likewise, evil is a term created by humans to describe the absence of God in the heart, so God did not create evil, it is the result of lacking of God's love in the human heart, just like cold comes from the absence of heat source and darkness comes from the absence of light ray ." The professor then asked: "Who are you, my young man?" The student replied: "Dear Professor, my name is Albert Einstein."

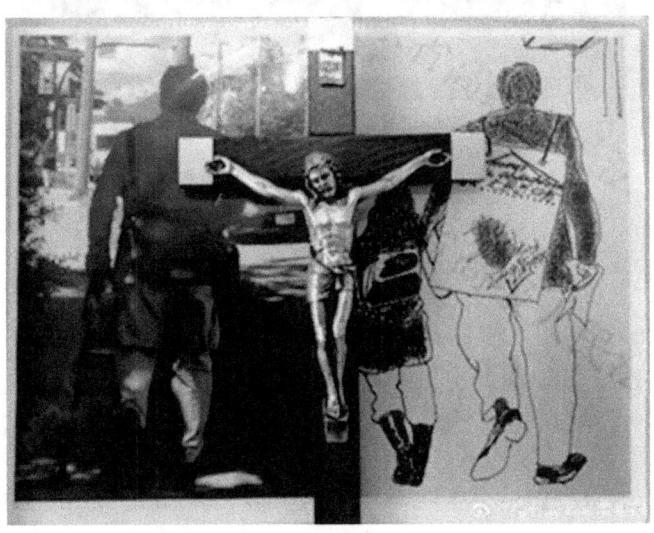

Official Weibo account: @A-Kidney-Stone-Baby's-Dad-Guo- Li (@结石宝宝父亲郭利)

# Preface

This is a documentary case, dictated and recorded by the victim part Guo, Li concerned. The whole story is full of ups and downs along with heartbreaking sessions. The protagonist Guo, Li was being framed and imprisoned from a high-profiled, promising young man to be a prisoner. After five years of unjust imprisonment, Guo still persevered and finally cleared his name on his own. What being recorded in this story, is a brave father, a real man from Beijing of China, who single-handedly fought against the abnormal social, cultural and non-rule of law "legal" environment there, demonstrating his deep love to the child as a father.

The cause of this case was that Guo, Li's daughter consumed a counterfeit American brand Scient@ baby formula in between 2006 and 2008 in Beijing, made by a Yashily Sino-US joint venture called Scient Infant Nutrition Co., Ltd. in Guangzhou since her six months after birth. Because the formula was added with an industrial raw material "melamine" that far more exceeded the tolerance level by 132 times, causing her daughter's severe harm with a multiple stones being diagnosed in her central collecting system of both kidneys, accompanied by the abnormalities in her urinary protein levels and blood routine specs. As the father of a baby, Guo, Li made legal claims against the Chinese baby formula manufacturer and its shareholder Yashily International in Guangdong Province, which was claimed to be "an American SCIENT"(meaning MERCY in English) advertisements broadcasting in China Central Television Station. During this process, the manufacturer Yashily colluded with the Guangdong judicial authorities to frame Guo and his family and later arrested him with a warrant across provinces, Guo was hence imprisoned for five years on charges of "extortion" in violation of the Chinese law.

Five years of wrongful imprisonment drove the protagonist Guo, Li from his heaven to hell. After being imprisoned, he persisted in not pleading guilty and suffered severe physical and mental tortures. Life in prison follows the collective bullying, abuse, beatings, hunger and loneliness...but Guo, Li never chooses to kneel down. He is like a huge tree, always maintaining a firm fighting spirit and strength with a faith remain firm and unshakable.

The victims of China "melamine" poisoned milk powder incident numbered in tens of millions. Guo, Li's experience was like a shining meteor falling from the stars, piercing the darkness; his actions made the parents of this huge number of being silenced victim families and their grown-up children keep quiet, feel ashamed of themselves one after another. But Guo still insists on fighting alone on the road of rights defense, so his background seems particularly grand.

From the time when Guo, Li was imprisoned by the "China Milk-Evil Forces" to the time he was released from prison, he continued to appeal and charge against them and was eventually re-trialed for twice, arraigned and acquitted. This process affected and promoted the safety and recognition of the entire Chinese food industry, making people around the world understand more about the Chinese environment and related judiciary just processes. Especially after Guo was acquitted, he firmly asked to hold the "China Milk-Evil Forces" accountable, where they colluded with the judiciary officials in doing the dairy business, concocted the unjust case and applied his entire independent rights defense process for a full "Guo, Li State Compensation Case" package in accordance with the law, which deeply affected legal professionals and public authorities at home and abroad, and raising a severe question or public concern.

In addition to completely exposing China's dark social environment, Guo, Li's unjust case also has a profound, positive impact on China's rule of law situation! It took several years for the Supreme Court, Ministry of Justice and other relevant departments to revise a number of judicial interpretations or regulations accordingly. This is the only revision of interpretations triggered by individual cases like the Guos in modern Chinese history; the results of Guo's case have a profound and far-reaching impact on those detained in the detention centers, and also on the living environment and human rights concerns for tens of millions of serving prisoners in and outside the Chinese prisons.

# Content

# Chapter 1.

# Incident of melamine-milk scandal broke, Guo began to defend his rights

I am the father of a child who was a victim of melamine-tainted milk powder incident in Beijing of China. And my name is Guo, Li. The background of my case is the Chinese melamine-tainted baby formula scandal that broke out in 2008.

In September 2008, China Central Television Station (CCTV), a China's central authoritative media, exposed a widespread scandal of baby formula produced by Chinese 22 large dairy companies including Hebei Sanlu Dairy Group, being found to contain melamine of excessive safety level. Melamine is an organic compound, white monoclinic crystal, almost odorless, and is a source of carcinogens on human. It is not allowed to be used in food processing or as food additives, but only allowed to be used as chemical industrial raw materials for the production of fertilizers, leather, paper, wood, synthetic resins and plastic products.

The above-mentioned Chinese and their "Sino-foreign joint venture" dairy companies located in the China territory deliberately added this chemical raw material melamine to the baby formula in order to increase the nitrogen content in their dairy products, thus passing off the higher protein quality that should be naturally contained in the milk powder source and passing it off as the higher one. After the scandal, on October 8th 2008, the Ministry of Health, the Ministry of Industry & Information Technology, the Ministry of Agriculture, the State Administration for Industry & Commerce, and the State Administration of Quality Supervision, Inspection and Quarantine jointly issued an announcement to formulate the regulations on adding melamine in the milk and dairy products, with a temporary limited melamine in baby formula should be less than 1 mg/kg. Anything higher than 1 mg/kg is deemed as an unsafe, substandard product and must be recalled from the market.

The General Administration of Quality Supervision, Inspection and Quarantine of China conducted tests on 68 batches of 22 well-known brands in baby formula industry including Sanlu, Yili, Yashily, Mengniu, Scient, Guangming, and Shengyuan. Various levels of excessive melamine content were detected in all of them. According to incomplete statistics, tens of millions of infants and young children have consumed these toxic melamine-tainted baby formula or milk powder. For a time, pediatric outpatient clinics in hospitals across the country were overcrowded by Infants and young children who had consumed "problem" dairy products, and they were led by their parents to the hospital for medical screening. Nearly 300,000 infants and young children were diagnosed with kidney stones and other subsequent symptoms.

As early as year 2006, once a poisoning incident occurred in Canada and the United States of North America, in which hundreds of pets of household died of kidney failure. The cause of a large number of pets' death was found to be of excessive levels of melamine contained in the exported pet food raw materials. The pet food company is headquartered in Canada, but its product ingredients are actually sourced from

China.

Subsequently, the Chinese government ordered the closure of those facilities of the food companies in China and revoked their business licenses. However, the penalties and results of this incident did not alert the relevant Chinese food industry businesses. What is more, melamine was again deliberately added as a food additive to the baby formula or dairy product used for their own infants and young children. Almost all dairy companies, without exception, were involved in this appalling tainted-milk scandal, which shocked the world.

It is very unfortunate that the "American Scient" Baby formula consumed by my daughter (nickname: Yiyi) is on the exposure list of melamine-tainted milk scandal announced by the General Administration of Quality Supervision, Inspection

Front and back photo of Scient / Yashily formula can

and Quarantine. This brand product claims to be from the United States, and the American flag and its company name in English are clearly printed on packaging of its products. I thought it was a top-grade "imported" formula, but during the random inspection, 4 batches of products were found to have exceeded the limit.

After getting the above announcement and news, my family and I were extremely anxious. After repeated inquiries and comparisons, I found that the Scient formula my daughter consumed was not included in these four batches of products. I JUST felt lucky, and even had a fluke-mind! At that time, its shareholder Yashily dairy claimed that except for the four batches of substandard products exposed by CCTV media, the rest of them were qualified. However, combined with my daughter's growth and development, my and the family's worries about this rhetoric have not diminished at all. Because just over a year ago in September 2008, I and my family discovered that our kid had the symptom of developmental delays, including obvious abnormalities in her weight, skin color, height and appetite etc..

Shortly after the domestic & foreign media continued to report on the fermented melamine scandal in China, we received a call from a community maternal and child health hospital in Haidian District designated by Beijing Municipal Health Bureau, informing us that it required a medical screening for infants & young children who had consumed the above-mentioned poisonous dairy brands. After receiving their call, I immediately took my daughter to the designated hospital for relevant health exams. After screening, the CT results showed that "Several punctate strong echoes were found & visible in the Central Collecting System of the victim's both kidneys", that is, my kid had punctate stones in both kidneys and was accompanied by turbid urine. In addition to the victim's physical examination and diagnosis, shortly after I was framed in Beijing by Yashily dairy in Guangdong province and arrested, imprisoned across provincial territories, my kid had another forced physical exam by the Guangdong Chaozhou Public Security Bureau (police station) at Beijing Children's Hospital, along with a further medical results showed that the kid having "abnormal urinary protein and blood tests routine data" symptoms.

The results of hospital examinations were like a huge bolt from the blue to me. I married late and had the kid late, and I didn't have this baby until I was nearly 38 years of age. My daughter is the pearl on my family's palm. Since my occupation and work nature was a freelance simultaneous interpreter (or conference interpreter), my annual income at that time was considered high-income in China and even in the capital Beijing, with an income of one million yuan. Therefore, I am able to provide better conditions for my kid as she grows up. Therefore, when we were choosing baby formula brands back then, my family and I chose the Scient brand, which was the most expensive and the best brand in Beijing's high-end dairy

The Scenes of Guo's team working as Conference Interpreter or SI for

major foreign Embassies events in China

market and was advertised on CCTV every day as "its dairy source imported from the United States."

This Scient brand of baby formula had the largest and

Pictures of Scient / Yashily's Advertisement represented by famous film figures on China Central Television, the national television station

most frequent placement during prime time on TV channels in China's capital and various major provinces and cities that year and in the years after I was wrongfully imprisoned. The Scient product spokespersons include well-known actors and actresses who are former RENYI director of the entertainment industry such as PU Cunxin, JIANG Wenli, YAO Chen and DONG Jie are all the most influential celebrities or Chinese CCP/national movie star faces at home and abroad. No one would have thought that a baby formula brand with such an "endorsement" background would be discovered, disclosed by me, in addition to being a counterfeit US dairy product, that it

would also add large doses of melamine, a food-banned industrial additive into the dairy product of Chinese infants and youngest children, in an attempt to murder them for their lifesaving money.

What is even more unacceptable is that the diagnostic instructions given by the Beijing Children's Hospital said that their doctors are unable and do not have any specific, mature and effective means of treating "melamine-related patients"; they can only wait until my child's condition becomes serious or we feel... If something is wrong with her, need go to the hospital for follow-up exam issue. My daughter was only one and a half years old at the time, and she developed kidney stones and her urine contained excessive amounts of protein, indicating that her kidney function was severely damaged. As her father, I can't imagine what her little body would look like in the future right after this ordeal! It's still unclear how serious her health problems will be in the future. How will she spend her future life along with such a harm? Knowing her being-

Screenshot of Scient's Advertisement

harmed history, my family and I can't really let it go.

Afterwards, I returned home in a huge worry. My mother (Xin, Hong) and I found all the purchase receipts and retained some of the problem formula cans and packaging of Yashily's (US) Scient product that had been purchased and consumed. After initially determining that my daughter had kidney stones and other symptoms due to the said poisonous melamine-tainted baby formula she had consumed, my family and I took her health examination report from a Beijing Hospital and the purchase receipts from Carrefour, WU-mart, and Wal-Mart markets to the Scient Beijing office. After rounds of twists and turns, we found this Scient Brand, a "Sino-US Joint Venture" baby food manufacturer based in Guangzhou and its major shareholder Yashily International headquartered in Chaozhou city, Guangdong province. Their customer service also responded with an "under-statement" to us, saying that don't worry sir, surely your child has not eaten those four batches of contaminated Scient formula that have been called back by the government.

"If you can show that you have consumed the four batches of baby formula that have been exposed and announced by the government, we (the Scient company) would consider reimbursing you for the medical expenses of the harmed child and providing relevant compensation to your family's victim...". The customer service also said that we (the victim children and family) would be compensated accordingly. The one-time compensation standard stipulated at that time for the giant "SanLu" dairy was 30,000 yuan for severe patients and 2,000 yuan for general patients. To be honest, my family cannot imagine or accept such an unreasonable and non-legal compensation standard!

According to a report from the Ministry of Health of China in December 2008, a total of 296,000 infants & children were affected by the melamine-milk scandal. This is just a general figure after its official diagnosis. The affected scope and actual data are far more than that, and should be 10 times higher than that of confirmed cases. The number of school-age children and families affected by the incident reaches tens of millions.

After ineffective and fruitless communication with the

Scient customer service for compensation issue, I personally went to Beijing Consumers' Association with my kid's hospital examination report and the Baby formula purchase receipts. During the meeting, the staff and director of the Consumers' Association expressed their disdain to me, said they couldn't do anything on it at all. In the process of reasoning with them, I felt that they did not take the tainted-milk incident seriously at all. It was just a trifle to them! The director was extremely

关于做好婴幼儿奶粉事件患儿相关疾病
医疗费用支付工作的通知

2009/2/26/08:41

【慧聪食品工业网】

慧聪网首页 > 食品工业行业 > 三聚氰胺问题奶粉 > 正文

关于做好婴幼儿奶粉事件患儿相关疾病医疗费用支付工作的通知

人社厅发〔2009〕10号

各省、自治区、直辖市劳动保障厅（局、卫生厅（局、新疆生产建设兵团劳动保障局、卫生局、各保监局：

为了做好婴幼儿奶粉事件患儿赔偿工作，现就患儿相关疾病医疗费用支付问题通知如下：

一、为保障医食用含三聚氰胺婴幼儿配方奶粉而患病婴幼儿的权益，由对此次事件负有责任的企业出资建立患儿医疗赔偿基金，并委托中国人寿保险股份有限公司代管，对患儿急性治疗终结后到18周岁以前可能发生的与此相关的疾病给予免费治疗。

二、患儿急性治疗终结后到18周岁以前，发生与食用含三聚氰胺婴幼儿配方奶粉而致的泌尿系统结石相关的以下疾病，可在儿童医院、妇幼保健院和二级以上综合医院进行治疗。

（一）残留结石及其合并症，如泌尿系统感染、血尿、梗阻等；

（二）结石梗阻后遗疾病，如高血压、泌尿系统感染等；

（三）肾衰及其合并症，如高血压、贫血等；

（四）术后合并症，如输尿管、尿道狭窄、膀胱输尿管返流、吻合口瘘并发肠粘连导致的肠梗阻等；

（五）尿路上皮癌。

三、医疗机构要以已建数据库为基础，进一步做好患儿相关疾病后续医疗有关信息的记录工作，并按照国家处理三鹿牌婴幼儿奶粉事件领导小组诊疗专家组会同中华医学会组织制订的《食用含三聚氰胺奶粉致泌尿系统结石患儿急性结石期后可能出现的相关疾病相关性判定要点》和相关疾病治疗规范，科学准确出具

Requirement for paying the medical expense

for kidney-babies from Ministry of Labors and Social Security

sarcastic and said, 'Why are you so anxious? Your kid are not the only one who have eaten this formula. Besides, there is no evidence to prove that there is something wrong with the formula your kid ate....'

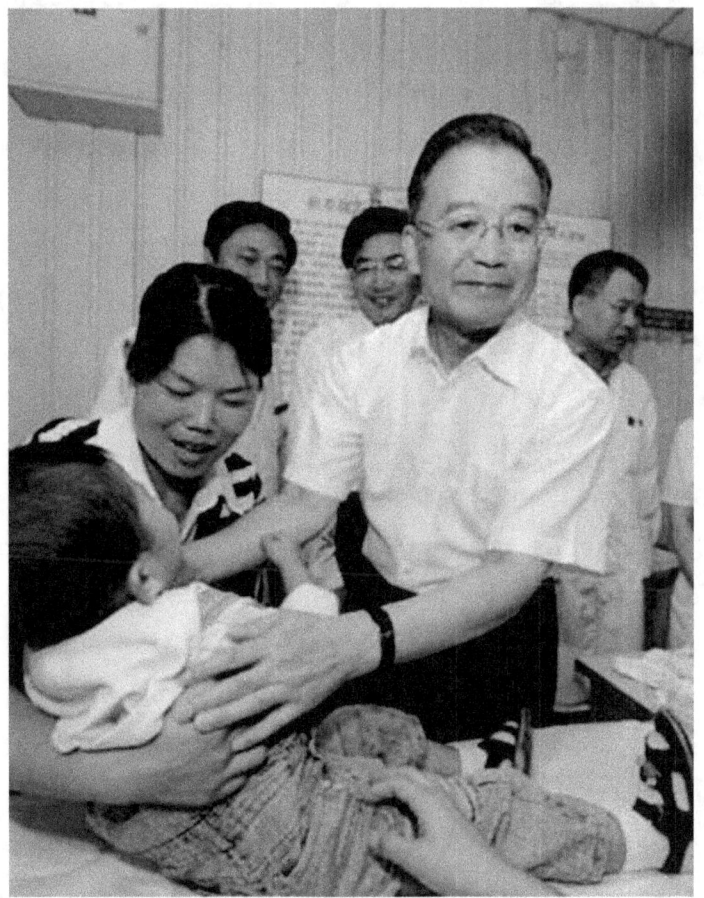

The Prime Minister Wen Jiabao with the sickened-baby

In my heart, I completely do not accept this irresponsible official attitude towards such a consumer infringement. At the same time, I deeply realized that in the eyes of these people, the children's health and future are simply irrelevant. I'm thinking maybe it's because their own children haven't eaten tainted-milk and dairy yet! When things have nothing to do with them or they thought that it had nothing to do with them, do they act so nonchalantly? What happened after that was the capacity of prevarication!

Then I called the Beijing Municipal Health Bureau, and the health director who received me (a middle-aged man) replied by saying that they had nothing to do with the matter. At the end of the call, he deliberately said to me: "What are you worried about? It's not only your kid (who was being harmed). This incident has affected so many families in China. We will have to die together!"

After repeatedly contacting the Beijing office of Guangdong Yashily Scient companies, as well as Beijing Consumers' Association, Health Bureau and other relevant departments to complain about the infringement and other claim issues, without positive results, I came up with the idea of finding a solution on my own and prepared to send the baby formula my kid consumes to undergo a national food quality standard and safety inspection. However, this process was with many twists and turns and challenging. During this disputed period, the YSL manufacturer's representative even made an extremely shameless statement saying that "You can choose not to buy our baby food product... If your kid doesn't eat it, she won't get sick from it..., correct?"

During this process, I tried every possible means to find

almost all private and designated state institutions with dairy product inspection qualifications in Beijing; however, almost all of the institutions rejected my request for a self-funded inspection. But with no way out and after my many phone calls and door-to-door consultations, I finally found the last but only official state designated agency willing to accept my private inspection at my own expenses, that is China National Food Quality and Safety Supervision & Inspection Center.

Immediately, I non-stop sent the remaining Scient infant formula at my home, which marked with different batches to the center, one of which was produced in March 2008 by the Sino-US joint venture Scient (Guangzhou) Infant Nutrition Food Co., Ltd.. Tests were conducted four times separately and the results were shocking. The three "Inspection Reports" obtained one after another showed that the actual measured values of melamine contained in my purchased baby formula submitted for inspection were 132.9 mg/kg, 25.5 mg/kg and 36 mg/kg respectively, far exceeding the national safety limit for the formula product. The safety limit of melamine substance value found in the baby formula should be ≤1mg/kg. And the test results show that the harm and risk caused by Scient product to my kid's health is severe and the consequences are fatal.

To make one hundred percent sure, I did several more tests, sending 2-3 batches of the formula samples for inspection each time, and conducted authoritative tests on multiple batches of Scient formula my kid had eaten. Among the test results, a sample with the highest melamine content exceeding the tolerance limit is the number of (Guo) XH0903420 with 132.9 mg/kg, over 133 times higher than the safety limit of <1 mg/kg. Also this sample is far exceeding the batches mentioned value previously disclosed, announced by media CCTV. The cost of inspection is also extremely dear. Each report obtained by giving a sample to the center for inspection at my own expense costs 3,000 to 5,000 yuan per product, and some even cost more than 10,000 yuan.

I was shocked when I obtained these official and authoritative baby formula inspection reports. First of all, I feel that I have been completely deceived by Yashily Scient. Secondly, I feel that they take children's health and life too much for granted. The manufacturer concealed the truth in quality problems of the product from us, they only admitted that the four batches of formula exposed by CCTV had harmful issues on babies. And they deceived me and said that the remaining batches of Yashily Scient product were all qualified with no contaminations. It is conceivable that even the quality of "US exported" dairy product for infants and young children had such serious fraud problems. Obviously, they do not take it seriously and only murder the consumers for their money.

I took the <Inspection Report> and once again found a director called LiMing of Yashily Scient (Guangzhou) Company in its Beijing office, told him that I checked their other batches of baby formula and found their additional product with

国家食品质量安全监督检验中心

检验报告单

样品名称：幼儿配方奶粉（第3段）　　商　标：澳贝佳 AUBANY＊

规格型号：700g/袋　　　　　　　　质量等级：合格品

生产日期或批号：39080317

生产单位：美国施恩婴幼儿食品国际有限公司授权施恩（广州）婴幼儿营养品有
限公司制造

送检单位：郭艺德（个人）　　　　　电　话：13910638592

样品编号：国 XH0903420　　　　　检验类别：委托检验

检验依据：GB/T 22388-2008《原料乳与乳制品中三聚氰胺检测方法》

| 检验项目 | 实测值 |
|---|---|
| 三聚氰胺 mg/kg | 132.9 |
| 以下空白 | |

备注：无

注：仅对所检样品负责。

收样日期：2009. 03. 31

检　样：林玉

批　准：

Inspection Report of Melamine Content of Yashily Scient baby
formula, From National Center for Food Quality and Safety
Supervision and Inspection

seriously exceeded melamine content. He asked me "How come?" Then I immediately showed him the "Report". After having read it, director LiMing completely disappeared. They sent another person from the northern China sales came to talk

广东雅士利集团股份有限公司不合格产品销毁清单

| 序号 | 物品名称 | 型号规格 | 批号 | 生产日期 | 数量 |
|---|---|---|---|---|---|
| 1 | 雅士利较大婴儿配方奶粉② | 25kg/包 | 2008年9月3日 | 2008年9月3日 | 染伍染拾叁包 |
| 2 | 雅士利婴儿配方奶粉① | 25kg/包 | 2008年9月1日 | 2008年9月1日 | 贰仟柒佰叁拾叁包 |
| | (以下空白) | | | | |
| | | | | | |
| | | | | | |
| | | | | | |
| | | | | | |

List of Defective Products for Destruction

of Guangdong Yashily Group

to me instead.

I further asked them: "Why do you say that except for the 4 batches of poisonous melamine-tainted formula exposed by CCTV, the other batches of your Yashily Scient's products are 100% safe? Since I have sent samples from multiple batches for quality inspection, and found almost every single batch of the tested formula seriously exceed the tolerance limit..." The newly replaced negotiator looked in pale and changed his face when he heard this, and explained: "This... maybe was an oversight by our company." Then, he also asked me tentatively "Do you have any other evidence?"

Indeed, for this I also did other investigations and

evidence collection; but when I saw that they did not really treat me with a serious negotiation attitude, and considering that I might encounter more challenges or problems in the subsequent rights defending, I tried to ask him: " In addition to those, what evidence do you still think is missing? What else do you think I need to come up with?" He thought for a moment and said: "Well, since YOU have these proof and evidences, we will give you a compensation in accordance with the "SanLu" company standard. I can compensate YOU with a one-time deal of 2,000 yuan." While speaking, he also gave me a copy of compensation form with the title of < An Open Letter to Victims of Sanlu Dairy Co.> and asked me to fill it out properly for a quick payment.

After reading it, I rejected him immediately with a firm reply: "I'm sorry, first of all I don't accept the 2,000 yuan as a full package of compensation. Since this amount (of compensation) is even not enough for me to cover all the money we paid for buying the formula in the past, as we have spent tens of thousands of yuan on your product in the past few years. Furthermore, I NOW have solid evidence that my child was harmed by having your formula products." In such a scenario, this negotiation naturally failed. However, in an unspoken intention, from here we have also reached to proceed to the next level in negotiations.

After that, I returned home and discussed with my family the approximate amount of compensation I needed to ask from the formula manufacturer. After our rough calculations, we found that the cost of actual purchasing and quality inspection of the claim was about 80,000 yuan. In addition to the time and energy spent by my family during the claim process and the subsequent general expenses of our kid may arise, we proposed a spiritual and moral compensation of 500,000 yuan to the manufacturer, with a total bid of 580,000 yuan. After hearing my word of this amount, the Yashily & Scient negotiators immediately said to us that it was impossible for them to accept the amount of 580,000 yuan. Their counter-plan is "buy one and pay ten", that is if I buy their defective product for 10,000 yuan, they can only compensate me 100,000 yuan. For this reference, they believe that the compensation amount of 580,000 yuan proposed by my family has no basis at all.

In fact, my family and I should have expected the outcome of similar negotiations. I think it doesn't matter if we can't reach an agreement. Anyway, I have enough evidence in my hand. If that doesn't work, I can still file a claim through the court proceedings in Beijing or Guangzhou. Then We did enough homework and asked someone go to the United States where the Scient USA of Yashily Int'l claims their brand register and its R&D location there, by doing our due diligence and preparing for supplementary collection of evidences.

The process of rights defense and struggle is very tortuous, so friends and families around me are not optimistic about it, especially my ex-wife GaoHong and her family were "forced to give up" the earliest they can!

The screenshot of advertisement including the quality slogan

"Mercy from America"... of Scient Baby Formula

in China Central Television and other major media

"Mercy from America"... This is the quality slogan of Scient Baby Formula promoted by China Central Television (CCTV)-6 and other major medias in China.

The Scient Company claims in its product promotion that their formula is manufactured and sold by Scient (Guangzhou) Infant Nutrition Co. Ltd., a Sino-foreign joint venture authorized by Scient Int'l Inc. USA. And it guarantees that this series of food product are of premium quality plus 100% imported ingredients or with original packaging. The content of the advertisement is even titled "Mercy from America, specially formulated with a certain ingredient containing A+ to improve children's immunity and stimulate their brain development..."

Because my job is simultaneous interpretation and business negotiation at international conferences, I have accumulated some overseas contacts in my daily work and life. So, based on some doubts, I launched my own investigation into the overseas business background of Yashily International in Guangdong, which owns the above-mentioned "Scient" brand and business in the US and the hidden story behind it. In addition to Beijing and Guangzhou of China at that time, my former foreign colleagues also traveled to and from the United States for this purpose, and soon we discovered anomalies at its US based headquarters for Scient, which it claimed to be owned.

After on-site inspections, telephone inquiries and with a written official response from the US FDA authorities, it was verified that the above-mentioned "Scient USA" International Inc. is actually a Chinese dairy company called Guangdong Yashily (with a "US director" named Frank Lin in the state of Texas) that only spent a few hundred dollar registered in the Lin's home of Sugar Land in Texas and another on the 1st floor of a parking lot in LA of California (which is abandoned, vacant with an accounting firm traces). They are actually empty shells (offshore companies) of Guangdong Yashily, and the products Scient applied for trade in USFDA database are the disposable medical gloves only.

Well, this "Sino-US joint venture" located in Guangzhou, Guangdong Province of China is not qualified to conduct R&D,

54

Filing Number: 800812339

**Texas Franchise Tax Public Information Report**
To be filed by Corporations, Limited Liability Companies (LLC), Limited Partnerships (LP),
Professional Associations (PA) and Financial Institutions

Tcode 13196 Franchise

Taxpayer number: 3 2 0 3 1 7 4 7 4 0 8   Report year: 2 0 1 6

SCIENT INTERNATIONAL (USA), INC.

13050 FORESTER CANYON LANE

SUGAR LAND          TX        77498

13050 FORESTER CANYON LANE, SUGAR LAND, TX, 77498
13050 FORESTER CANYON LANE, SUGAR LAND, TX, 77498

1000000000015

FRANK LIN          President      08/25/2016      ( 626 )  291 - 8200

Texas Comptroller Official Use Only

formulate and manufacture of infant food under the USFDA regulations, as they have widely publicized in advertisements and online media, and is required to be certified and approved by the USFDA for its authorization and compliance. In essence, Scient USA is just an offshore international company that, although legally registered in the US, operates illegally in China without the approval from the USFDA.

However, what its major shareholder Yashily in Guangdong has promoted about its U.S. shareholders, the product R&D center and even its overseas sales are actually groundless and false propaganda. As for the only managing director of Scient USA named Mr. FRANK LIN, I found his social security number in the United States and talked with him on the phone. In fact, he is a Chinese American who immigrated to the United States in his earlier years, and may be a relative of Zhang Litian, the former NPC Congressman, Chairman of Yashily International when it was listed in Hong Kong.

It is worth mentioning that during this period, I found the person in charge of the US Food and Drug Administration (USFDA) in China office through the embassy, and thus inquired about the situation of this Scient company. The USFDA finally issued a written certificate through the embassy saying: After checking the registry, searching in the database, we did not find the information about the "Scient International Infant-food Inc., USA", but from the similar company names registered as "Scient" in the database, we found a company called "Scient International Inc., USA". It is not a formula company or a R&D company for formula, but a trading company that sells medical disposable gloves to the United States. When my colleagues, friends and the USFDA personnel went to the site to check this Scient's homeland office, they found that it was not a real business premises at all, and there was no formula production facilities there, but an empty room at the parking lot.

In the room with No. 2079E, where it was empty on the

An Office of Scient Int'l (Infant food) Inc., in USA

ground floor of a parking lot building at Monterey Park, LA of California, Yashily Scient of Guangdong in China successfully registered the so-called Scient Int'l (Infant Food) Inc., USA. It was precisely because of the news about my cross-border investigative action and solid evidence collection that Yashily and its Scient (Guangzhou) joint venture in Guangdong panicked, and then they came to me very unusually and proactively.

Chapter 2.

# Negotiating a compensation package under the guise of being framed by Yashily

In the Chinese "melamine" incident, the most influential one was the "famous" domestic brand Sanlu milk powder. After the incident was exposed, Sanlu Dairy Group's reputation was immediately discredited, its Chairwoman Tian Wenhua became China's "Poisonous Dairy Queen" and even was given the name of "the Sinner of China's Dairy Industry." Tian later was criminally charged, detained by the Chinese public security department (police) after the incident was exposed, and was eventually sentenced to life imprisonment by the local court in accordance with the law.

Melamine has had a huge impact on the dairy industry in China and around the world. At that time, almost all brands of domestic milk powder in China were spurned by consumers, their sales suffered a heavy setback, and their credibility was completely ruined by the scandal. In addition to milk powder, other foods containing milk powder ingredients have also been implicated; the most famous of which is the "Golden Emperor" chocolate produced by a large Chinese state-owned enterprise called COFCO(China National Cereals, Oils and Foodstuffs Corporation), and a "Cadbury" series of brands from the UK's largest candy company, were also severely affected. For example, shortly after the melamine incident, the said local famous Golden Emperor brand chocolate quickly disappeared from the 2nd position of high-end market in China's domestic chocolate sales ranking list. The Cadbury brand has also urgently recalled more than ten of its chocolate products from countries other than the mainland China!

The industry decline and deteriorating situation continued for many years, and even up to now of 2024 when this book is almost finished in Chinese, it cannot be truly reversed or gets better. At present, Chinese parents raising infants and young children, regardless of whether they have the financial conditions or not, will try their family best to buy various brands of high-quality baby formula in person or through global purchasing agents from nearby Hong Kong and Australian markets and even from distant retail markets in continents of Europe, North America through various overseas connecting channels. This has resulted in frequent shortages and sold-out of baby formula market supply for Chinese consumers in the above-mentioned countries and regions. Due to the heavy influence of Chinese consumers' global purchasing agents, pharmacies like in Germany, New Zealand, Australia, the United States and Canada, etc. have successively

Picture of drug stores' notice in Hong Kong

implemented sales policies that limit the purchase of two cans per person at a time. After that, the Hong Kong SAR government implemented strict purchase restrictions for mainland Chinese consumers. According to its (by)-laws, the mainland residents can only purchase a maximum of two 900g cans of milk powder per day. Violators may be fined up to HK$500,000 and imprisoned for two years upon conviction.

The Tsunami-like earthquake caused by melamine-tainted dairy scandal not only put all dairy companies in China in a big trouble, but also triggered a massive rights defending actions and protests among the victimized family groups. The news media also paid continuous attention to and offered some followed-up reports on such consumer "WeiQuan" (rights defending) incidents.

Due to my daily consumption habits and the awareness nature of my foreign affairs work, I have obvious advantages over other victims during my 16 years of rights defending struggle. First of all, my family and I usually have the habit of keeping shopping receipts, and their retention time is often more than three years. In addition, the products we purchase, such as baby formula, will be kept (samples) both uneaten and eaten in original packaging to prepare for future quality problems. As far as I know, many victimized families have not kept their shopping receipts, nor have they kept any samples of problematic products for their own inspection. As a result, they are unable or do not have the essential conditions to submit the formula for inspection, and therefore lose the advantage or opportunity to protect their legitimate rights and interests of defense.

Based on my born-in-nature rights-defending qualities, as well as other advantages and conveniences such as good bilingual proficiency, negotiation skills and financial arrangements, I became the target of many domestic or international media. The progress of my rights-related defense has also been covered, tracked and followed continuously by them since 2008.

It may be that the above-mentioned media exposure and follow-up caused panic in Yashily and its Scient US joint venture in Guangzhou. After learning that I had investigated the background of their companies, and that I had a written certificate from the embassy and the USFDA office, as well as their formula's "Product Inspection Report" in my hand, the persons in charge of their Guangdong Yashily Int'l and director of Northern China Sales Region from Scient GZ Company decided to visit my family in Beijing and also agreed on a time and place there for holding our further meeting and negotiation.

I received a call early in the morning on June 13th, 2009 and our negotiating parts made an appointment to meet at a teahouse above a Bank of China business outlet nearby the Cuigong Hotel in Haidian District of Beijing. In addition to Duan Genghui, director of Northern China Sales, members of Yashily and Scient also participated in the negotiations, including Chen Minhui, director of external affairs of Yashily Int'l. In addition to the claims' description and proposed amounts, the major issue of the negotiation was more about the shut up (or hush) money and their use of the agreement that Yashily wanted to apply to bind my family.

Negotiations lasted the whole day from early morning to early night. Duan Genghui, the main negotiator of defendant part, self-claimed to be from Taiyuan of Shanxi Province held this talk, from time to time, he would need to enter and exit the teahouse once for about a quarter of an hour. His behavior was quite strange; and for every negotiation issue or detail, he would use his mobile phone to lend cover for leaving the teahouse. It seemed that there is some kind of discussion going on in private with "another person" out there. During this period, people seemed to feel that there was an unexplained murderous intention looming around us! However, at the last moment of this meeting when the teahouse was about to close, the two parts finally reached an agreement on the amount of claims and related issues and even added a clause regarding its confidentiality.

The amount of claims was finally negotiated to 400,000 yuan. Actually I am quite dissatisfied with this result. Is my daughter's health and future only worth the claimed 400,000 yuan? However, this one year's rights defending process also made me exhausted both physically and mentally. In the eyes of those outsiders, this amount may already be astronomical, according to Tao Xin, my kid's grandma-in-law! After all, the Sanlu Dairy Group, which was the scapegoat and involved in the melamine-tainted milk business scandal, only offered compensation ranging from 2,000 to 20,000 yuan. If there is evidence that proves the direct cause of kid's death arising from the baby formula, a 200,000 yuan would be paid to the dead victim. Even my ex-wife thought this way at the time: Our kid was harmed by tainted baby formula, and the whole family was under tremendous pressure. My ex-wife was so anxious about this that she had to abort herself another baby during expectancy. My mother Xin, Hong is also very worried about her grandchild's health, but also feels deep sorry for the time and energy I have put into defending my kid's rights. At this moment, all the family members hope it will end as soon as possible.

After the terms of the agreement were finalized, the two parts opened a special bank account for my family in the Bank of China business outlet below our negotiation teahouse. Then,

Beijing Youth Daily's news on the baby formula of Scient is not imported as they advertised

almost at the last minute before the bank closed, Yashily Int'l in Guangdong used a private bank account outside Beijing to deposit 400,000 yuan in cash into my family newly opened account.

The main content of the supplementary agreement to this settlement is that I should keep the payment confidential. In

# 中国乳制品工业协会

### 关于对雅士利《请中国乳制品工业协会出具雅士利集团股份有限公司已经履行三聚氰胺事件赔偿义务函》的复函

雅士利集团股份有限公司：

贵公司《请中国乳制品工业协会出具雅士利集团股份有限公司已经履行三聚氰胺事件赔偿义务函》已收悉。现复函如下：

2008 年发生的"问题奶粉"事件，涉及到患儿 29 万人之多，包括冻患在内有 22 家责任企业。为了使受到伤害的患儿能得到经济赔偿，由 22 家企业按承担的责任大小向相关机构一次性交付一定数额的赔偿金，再由相关机构统一对患儿发放，企业不直接对患儿赔偿。患儿赔偿金除一次性对患儿进行赔偿外，还拿出部分资金设立患儿基金，为患儿在 18 周岁之前治病支付医疗费。

贵公司作为三聚氰胺事件 22 家赔偿企业之一，与我协会签定了《委托协议》。并于 2008 年 12 月 20 日前，按照要求的数额和时间交付了赔偿款 4314.21 万元，如期履行了赔偿责任。我协会于 2008 年 12 月 25 日将 22 家企业交付的赔偿款汇至全国 32 个省、市、自治区，由各地有关单位于 2009 年 1 月 15 日前将赔

Yashily Compensation package paid confirmation

issued by China Dairy Product Industry Association

fact, when I thought about it later, it seemed that the 400,000 yuan provided by Yashily Int'l was not compensation for the children and family, but more like a "hush payment." Yashily believes that their compensation of 400,000 yuan to my family is already the highest amount of claims. As far as I know, there were dozens of victim families like mine who made collective actions against Yashily. Perhaps for the benefit of the defendant, they asked me to keep the compensation agreement of both parts concerned confidential, but I don't know if it was due to their negligence or not, the agreement signed by both parts did not mention that I as the victim side could not expose other content to the public or accept media interviews.

A few days later, Yashily Int'l officially admitted to the public in national newspapers such as Beijing Daily, Beijing Youth Daily, and Beijing Evening News and on Internet regarding its status as a "fake foreign brand": the Scient Baby Formula they produced is not a truly foreign brand, and its advertising has misled Chinese consumers. The Scient Company has publicly apologized to consumers for its deceptive behavior...

Just when I thought the road to rights defending might be coming to an end, on June 25th 2009, Beijing TV station "Beijing Youth• Channel" broadcast a program about a rights defender who was victim of poisoned milk powder, entitled <A Man Makes Scient Formula Bow Its Head>. The broadcast of this program completely changed the path of my life!

It is said that Guangdong Yashily Int'l Group, the holding company behind the Joint Venture called Scient Guangzhou, was preparing to go public in Hong Kong in 2009. In order not to affect its listing process, Yashily had no choice but to reach the above-mentioned "compensation" agreement with my family and publicly apologize to consumers across the country through the media. While I was safeguarding the rights, I provided my kid's "Product Inspection Report", which was 133 times higher than the tolerance level, free of charge to the nearly fifty families of the victims of Yashily & Scient baby formula product, "a class action lawsuit case in 2009" which was already on the verge of losing their rights & case. Their agents and lawyers soon successfully signed a "collective compensation" agreement with Yashily of Guangdong, involving millions of yuan in harmed case of claims.

However, it was later learned that after excluding the legal team's agency fees, the amount of compensation paid to each individual victim of family was pitifully small! The amount of compensation ranges from a few thousand to tens of thousands of yuan per household. As for this handful of compensation, Yashily and Scient also stated in the "secret agreement" with its legal team representing the victims that it was a one-time compensation. The family members of the victims did not keep valid shopping receipts for purchasing the faked product, and they did not think about, nor did they have the conditions to, submit for inspection of the melamine content in the formula they purchased and consumed that caused harm to their children. Therefore, the family members of the above-mentioned victims could only, and reluctantly accept the reality, they stopped legal action and ceased fire completely.

Screenshot of the TV program

&lt;A Man Makes "Scient" Formula Bow Its Head&gt;

Compared to them who tried to file a class sue, the claims I received seemed like a sky-high price to those by-standers.

After receiving the compensation, I began to return to my normal work and life. However, when the Beijing TV program &lt;A Man Makes "Scient" Formula Bow Its Head&gt; was broadcast, it seemed that a disaster struck me strangely and quickly.

The program &lt;A Man Makes "Scient" Formula Bow Its Head&gt; gave a detailed introduction to my rights defending experience. At the end of this story, the host also added a monologue: "The victimized consumer Mr. Guo will continue to defend his rights." It was this word that made Yashily Int'l Group feel threatened and panicked. They believe that the previous claimed amount of 400,000 yuan is already a sky-high offer! That's the price they have to pay in order to go public in the Hong Kong SAR. The last word added by Beijing TV Station made Yashily and Scient feel that I had gone back on my family promise and failed to act in accordance with the compensation agreement.

In fact, this word was said by the TV station, not me. Moreover, Beijing TV Station had already followed and interviewed me before I reached an agreement with Yashily. The production of this program requires enough time, from interviewing, recording, editing, reviewing to broadcasting, which takes about half a year to have it completed. Due to the delay in the broadcast of the program, Yashily felt that they were fooled by me. I caught them off guard, and they thought that their compromise with my family did not achieve the effect of eliminating the impact on its launching of IPO in Hong Kong. Because the broadcast of this program also became the key evidence for the Chaozhou Court of Guangdong Province to convict me of "extortion", the Guangdong Public Security (police) and Prosecutor's' Dept. regarded this TV word as my "criminal" motivation.

This program was broadcast on Beijing TV Station. Yashily Int'l Group immediately bombarded me with phone calls. I can't remember how many calls they made. I thought the road to claims with Yashily and Scient was over after signing the "settlement" agreement. Moreover, due to my busy work backlog and my previous rights defending activity, I had no time to pay attention to nearly a hundred harassment calls from them like this.

Three days after the program aired, on June 28th 2009, Yashily Int'l Group once again sent Duan Genghui, Director of Scient North China Sales to appear. After he arrived in Beijing,

雅士利·蒙牛构陷谋害郭利
第一犯罪小组成员

造假案律师·吴晓南
（汕头）

谋害策划·张利钿 *
（潮州）

构陷执行·段爽惠 *
（山西）

Some members of the framing case in Yashily company

he not only visited my home several times in person, but also brought some gifts to show us his sincerity, but he was still rejected. After being rejected, Duan was not discouraged and continued to call and send me text messages, asking us to consider meeting and make requests to them.

At the same time, my ex-wife's best friend from Air China in Beijing, Zhang Lin, also made an unexpected appearance. This woman is still a thorn in my heart, and I still don't want to mention her. She may have colluded with Yashily Int'l Group very early in order to do Yashily's advertising business. During the process of defending my rights, she kept probing and instigating me, asking my ex-wife to prove my "criminal" intention and destroy our mutual trust, marriage and family life. After I was arrested by the Chao'an County Police, as an outsider, Zhang also fully cooperated with the police in Chaozhou city and Chao'an county of Guangdong Province to search my home in Beijing and act illegally as their witness. As a past friend of my ex-wife, Zhang participated in the entire process of Yashily Int'l frame-up of me and made an "indelible" contribution on this.

On the other side of the concocted case, Wu Xiaonan, the former secretary of the board of directors of Yashily International Group and the current company's legal counsel at the time, flew from Guangzhou to the Chao'an County Public Security Dept. in Chaozhou City of Guangdong Province at almost the same time to report the case, saying: "Guo was interviewed by the media, threatening to create an uncontrollable situation and extorting money from their companies".... In other words, the case reported by Yashily Group to the Chaozhou County Police is a fact of a case that has not yet occurred, and the place of reporting (Chao'an) has nothing to do with the so-called crime facts in the future. It is neither the place where the crime occurred (in Beijing), nor the location of the victim (in Guangzhou) or the suspect (in Beijing).

On June 29th 2008, I was being interviewed by CCTV's <People's Stories> or Baixing Gushi program at Cuigong Hotel in Haidian District of Beijing. At this moment, Duan Genghui called me again. This is the first time I've ever answered a call from Yashily Scient. He asked me: "Hello, Mr. Guo. I am Duan Genghui, the negotiator of Yashily & Scient. Do you think we can meet today in Beijing?" I said: "No, Sorry I can't make that. I am with my mother, it is not convenient." Duan Genghui said

"Then call your mother and let's meet together." I asked him: "Why are we meeting?" Duan replied: "We want to hear your more opinions and suggestions. If you are not satisfied, we can meet and talk again. "This time, I still rejected Duan's request to meet us.

Director Duan did not give up. He then made two more phone calls to explain that Zhang Litian, Chairman of Yashily & Scient, had come from Guangdong province. After their Chairman arrived in Beijing, I could directly tell them any ideas we had and they would all be willing to listen to my family's voice. With such a sincere invitation from their companies, we met at Cuigong Hotel in Haidian District of Beijing on the evening of June 29th 2009.

At that time, I faced their phone invitations and door-to-door visits from Yashily & Scient companies. After being rejected several times, they still showed their sincerity and extended an "olive branch" under such circumstances. I felt that there was something fishy, but I couldn't figure it out for the moment that something went wrong. At that time, reporters from the CCTV news channel "People's Stories" (or Baixing Gushi) were filming and producing my rights defending album. I thought this might be an opportunity to fully compensate my family and the kid.

That night, I and my mother XinHong, together with Chen Minhui, Director of External Affairs of Yashily, and Duan Genghui, Director of China North Region Sales of Scient, who were the special representatives of Yashily International Board Chairman Zhang Litian, met in the hotel lobby. Chen said straight to the point: "If you are still dissatisfied, including your family members, just feel free to tell us. We are willing to listen and we are willing to summarize." After repeated inducements by Chen and Duan, I asked: Should Yashily & Scient consider these compensations for my lost work pay for the past one year and my kid's lifelong critical illness insurance? Chen and Duan replied on the spot that they could make all of our requests, but we couldn't just say them verbally. We had to write them down.

I didn't think about it that deeply at the time, so I told them: "No, you can ask them (life insurance co.) and then you can calculate it yourself. Look at my lost wages and income for the past one year, which is almost one million yuan, and there are life-long living expenses claimed for our kid, where the cost of future living is almost over one million yuan, plus our kid's life insurance for major harmed diseases like kidney, heart and stomach is about one million yuan, we have already checked with the China Life insurance company, and the total cost is more than 3 million yuan."

After Chen Minhui and Duan Genghui listened to my explanation, they asked us to write a list with a pen and explain the reasons for our additional claims of compensation. After we wrote and revised it according to their wishes, Chen and Duan asked my mother XinHong and me to sign our names on this paper. I didn't think about it at the time, so I told them "There is no need for us to sign, aren't you here just to understand the situation anyway? Now you are asking us for additional request for our compensation issue. If we are completely satisfied, then we think it is the update and the amount that we resubmit for now, you just go back and talk to the board of directors and the chairman. There is no need to sign on this!" Both Chen and Duan replied firmly, "No...no...no, if you don't sign on this paper, we won't know who wrote it actually." We think what they said makes sense... Right after their repeated requests, my mother XinHong and I decided to sign on the updated list.

After that, these requests and documents that we signed on paper at their request also became important evidence of my "extortion". The content of the initial police report made by Wu Xiaonan, the legal counsel of Yahily & Scient Companies, was the program broadcast on Beijing TV station with the last word of host saying "Guo said that he would continue to defend his rights...", plus the phone recordings and negotiation recordings before and after the claim negotiation, together with our asked, additional claim application signed by my mother and I.

Obviously, such evidence does not meet the necessary conditions to convict me of "extortion". When the case could not be filed by them, Yashily's Chen Minhui and Duan Genghui, as well as their lawyer Wu Xiaonan, had no choice but to continue to cooperate with the Chao'an County Police of Guangdong province. On July 1st 2009, Duan Genghui took the initiative to call me four times and sent me text messages.

The next day, Duan Genghui sent me another text message, called me twice, and repeatedly asked me to meet them. So we met at the Yuantong Hotel on Ping'an Street in the West 2nd Ring Road of Beijing. At the insistence of Chen Minhui and Duan Genghui, we made some written demands for supplementary compensation, which were the specific

全国召回不合格批次产品销毁清单

| 品名 | 规格 | 批号 | 数量（件） | 折合重量（吨） |
|---|---|---|---|---|
| 金装婴儿配方奶粉II | 400g*12 | 5-29 | 791 | 3.797 |
|  | 400g*12 | 6-3 | 883 | 4.238 |
|  | 400g*12 | 6-17 | 643 | 3.086 |
|  | 400g*12 | 6-27 | 839 | 4.027 |
| 金装较大婴儿配方奶粉 | 400g*12 | 7-20 | 573 | 2.750 |
|  | 400g*12 | 7-28 | 880 | 4.224 |
|  | 400g*12 | 8-16 | 1390 | 6.672 |
| 金装幼儿配方奶粉 | 400g*12 | 8-1 | 1367 | 6.562 |
|  | 400g*12 | 8-?1 | 2761 | 13.253 |
| 新配方婴儿配方奶粉II | 400g*12 | 5-15 | 740 | 3.552 |
| 优怡女士特殊配方奶粉 | 400g*12 | 7-9 | 89 | 0.283 |
|  | 400g*12 | 6-3 | 69 | 0.283 |
| 中小学生特殊配方奶粉 | 400g*12 | 7-15 | 79 | 0.379 |
|  |  | 合计： | 11064 | 53.107 |
|  | 件数合计大写： | 壹万壹仟零陆拾肆 | | 件 |
|  | 重量合计大写： | 伍拾叁壹零柒 | | 吨 |

单位负责人：

现场监督部门：

市质监局：

市食品安全委员会办公室：

县质监局：

县食品药品监督管理局：

二〇〇九年一月二十日

Recall List of Defective Products for Destruction

Total 53.107 tons

details of the claims of three million yuan. I listed my lost work expenses for this year's rights defending, my kid's serious illness insurance, and the details of our family life-long security compensation in the future.

Since this supplementary compensation request is reasonable, it still does not meet the standards for criminal cases filed by the local police dept. It must have been under the professional guidance of the Chao'an County case-handling police officers that the next day on July 3rd 2009, Duan Genghui once again texted and called us to meet at the Yuantong Hotel, and asked us to write another document. On July 4th, Duan Genghui invited me to continue negotiations at the same Hotel and asked to revise and supplement the compensation materials. On July 5th, Duan Genghui continued to follow up with me on the issue of compensation. On the other side, right after another negotiator, Chen Minhui met with us, he quickly went to Chao'an County with the written materials signed by us and submitted the so-called evidence of my extortion to the Chao'an County Police.

On July 6th, 2009, the most important figure in the "Guo Li extortion case", Zhang Litian, Chairman of Yashily International Group and Member to the Chinese National People's Congress, also moved immediately from behind the scenes to the front. He had two direct phone calls with us between negotiations.

After the phone call, Zhang Litian, one of the reporters to

the police, immediately went to Chao'an County in person and submitted the recording of our call conversation to the police dept. in his hometown as evidence of extortion.

During the week from June 29th to July 6th 2009, the existing evidence collected by Yashily Int'l on its own initiative to induce my family to apply another claim of compensations was still not enough for their public security dept. to convict me of extortion. Therefore, Duan Genghui negotiated with my family in "good" faith and kept it going on. They repeated reminding us to write down specific reasons for our further claim. They emphasized that the more comprehensive, touching, and profound the reasons of claim we write to them, the higher the amount of compensation we would get.

On July 7th, Duan Genghui and we met again at the Yuantong Hotel of Beijing. Under the advice of the bribed case investigators from local police dept. and Yashily's legal counsel Wu Xiaonan, Duan Genghui as the major negotiator, used his ingenious and superb negotiation skills to induce us to add another reason for our claim, which was that my ex-wife Gao Hong suffered from excessive anxiety during the process of defending her rights with an unexpected abortion for this. After adding this reason of claim, they believed that the conditions for filing a "criminal" case against me should be sufficient. So Duan went back immediately from Beijing to Chao'an County of Guangdong Province the next day and submitted the last but new evidence he collected from us to the police.

So far for exactly 10 days, they pretended to be

Pregnancy and lactation formula packaging of Scient,

marked as imported material from the USA

negotiating with us and had already reported the case to the police. Then according to the standards and requirements for filing a criminal case against me, they constantly changed their strategies and negotiation skills, adding and improving all the necessary content or evidence against our "extortion".

Two days later, on July 11th 2009, Duan Genghui contacted me again for compensation update. After having three phone calls with us, on July 18th Duan added the recordings of these calls as updated evidence to the Chao'an County Police.

After Duan Genghui returned to Guangzhou, and due to my work schedules, I have been negotiating with American business representatives in the cities of Shanghai, Hangzhou, Suzhou, and Wuxi on a contract to purchase solar power panels for North America. At this moment, Duan still calls me frequently and asks me to meet. On July 21st, Duan insisted on asking me for a meeting, I said I was on a business trip, and the location of the business trip was not fixed. He said it didn't matter, we could make an appointment on that. We agreed twice on the time and place to meet each other, but for an unknown reason, Duan did not keep the promise as he used to do. Moreover, Duan did not behave as cheerfully as before during the conversations. Instead, he kept changing his reasons to deal with me. Because I was busy with work at the time, Duan failed to make appointments several times. And I was tired of dealing with him like this, and finally got angry with him and said: "If you don't compensate us, I will expose it to the media, and I will contact the World Health Organization..." some words like this.

On the evening of July 22nd, Duan Genghui and I originally planned to meet at the Holiday Inn in Xiacheng District, Hangzhou of Zhejiang province, and agreed to hand over the three million yuan as our additional claim of compensation to my mother and me the following day.

Guo, Li shows the place where he was arrested in Hangzhou, Zhejiang

That night, my mother XinHong, my American colleagues and I went out from our hotel for a light snack. The snack session lasted until early in the morning. On our way back to the hotel, in the middle of the road in Hangzhou, my mother and I were suddenly stopped by two cars driving quickly towards us. Because it was so dark at night and the vehicle was unmarked, we had no idea on who these people were. At that time, several people rushed out of the cars, surrounded us, grabbed my hands, put the handcuffs on and said to me: "You are under arrest, just come with us." They quickly escorted me into the car. Because the vehicle that stopped us was not a police car, and the people who took me away did not wear police uniforms or show their work IDs. At that moment, I saw my mother shouting, and panicked by the sudden situation.

She shouted on the streets of Hangzhou: "HELP, Come and SAVE my son!" Because of my mother's crying with shouting, the plainclothes also took away my mother's handbag containing her chronic medicines. I was arrested and taken to a major police detention center under the Xiacheng District Public Security Bureau of Hangzhou. It wasn't until the

Solar eclipse of July 22, 2009

Map

police in the interrogation room, at my fierce fight back and legal request, returned my mother's medical kit to her who was still calling for help on the street that my mother later knew that it was the police in Hangzhou of Zhejiang province and the

108

### 接受刑事案件登记表

编号：A445121140600 2009070001

| 报案人 | 姓名 | 吴晓南 | | 性别 | 男 | 年龄 | 岁 | 住址 | |
|---|---|---|---|---|---|---|---|---|---|
| | 单位 | | | 联系方式 | 13827338982 | | 案件来源 | 案临报警 | |
| 移送单位 | | | | 承办人 | | | 电话 | | |

报案内容（发案时间、地点、简要过程、涉案人基本情况、受害情况等）：

2009年6月30日10时，吴晓南到我队报称：受广东雅士利集团股份有限公司委托，前来雁安县公安局刑侦大队报案。今年5月份，有一名叫郭利的北京籍男子称其女儿郭艺涵因食用雅士利公司旗下的"施恩公司"的婴儿奶粉检查出肾脏"点状结晶、强回音的症状"，向施恩公司和雅士利公司索赔58万元人民币（按国家规定雅士利公司没有向患儿直接赔偿的义务）。雅士利公司派员与郭利联系，告知上述情况，要求郭利通过申请向国家有关部门办理赔偿手续，郭利予以拒绝。我公司要求郭利提供相关证明材料，并带其女儿到医院进一步检查确证，郭利均予以拒绝。郭利利用媒体报道歪曲事实，对施恩公司的产品销售造成恶劣的负面影响，导致施恩公司产品销售急剧下降，损失极大。雅士利公司被迫无奈，于2009年6月13日与郭利协商，达成协议由雅士利公司赔偿郭艺涵40万人民币，并支付了该赔偿款项。赔偿协议达成并支付赔偿款后，郭利又以此事件造成其妻子流产、其本人的误工费、女儿到终生保险费和生活保障费为借口，以接受媒体采访报道，造成无法控制的局面相威胁，向雅士利公司索要人民币300万元。

领导批示：

初查。

2009年7月8日

处理结果：

经初查，符合立案条件。经局领导批准立为雅士利集团股份有限公司被敲诈勒索案侦查。

2009年7月11日

| 接警单位 | 雁安县公安局刑事警察大队县城中队 | 接警地点 | 雁安县公安局刑事警察大队县城中队 |
|---|---|---|---|
| 接警人员 | 刘锐佳 | 接警时间 | 2009年6月30日10时0分 |

Police records of Chao'an Police station on Guo, Li's framing case,

retrieved from Guangdong Court

police from the Chaozhou and Chao'an county of Guangdong province. The thing was, the police from Hangzhou of Zhejiang province actually cooperated with the ones from Guangdong province to come to Zhejiang Province to arrest me. The day right before that night of my arrest developed a total eclipse of the sun, and the sky of Hangzhou the day was completely in darkness.

At the detention center of Xiacheng District Public Security Bureau of Hangzhou, the police from Guangdong conducted a overnight interrogation of me. They said that they wanted to take me away from Zhejiang to Guangdong Province because I was suspected of extortion on Yashily and Scient there; in exchange, my mother XinHong could return to Beijing. At night the next day, I was handcuffed and escorted by four police officers from Guangdong to Hangzhou Xiaoshan Airport of Zhejiang province. On the plane heading to Fujian province, four police officers surrounded me in the last row of the plane seats to control me. During this period, I was not allowed to eat or drink or even use the bathroom. A few hours later, our plane arrived at Xiamen Int'l Airport in Fujian Province. As soon as the plane stopped, seven or eight more plainclothes came up and escorted me into a special van. In this way, I was "magically" captured from Zhejiang province to a place called Chao'an County of Guangdong province that I had never heard of in my life before. On the high way driving to Chao'an, a policeman said to me weirdly: "After you arrive at the destination, just cooperate with us for investigation three to five days, once the case is investigated clearly, you will be freed according to the laws."

After I was arrested and taken to the Chao'an County Public Security Bureau in Guangdong, I was again taken into a completely enclosed interrogation room. There were no windows in this room, so I couldn't tell the difference between day and night. Another team of police asked me to sit on a typical Chinese TIGER chair, where tortures and inhumane restrictions are in good place. While at the interrogation table five meters away from me, the interrogation officers from the task force were already sit-waiting.

The interrogator revealed that they were policemen from the Criminal Investigation Brigade of the Chao'an County of Guangdong. After hearing this info., I was somewhat confused. I further asked him: "Where is Chao'an?" I knew Chaoyang District of Beijing, because I am from Beijing, the case should be held within the jurisdiction of Beijing that has jurisdiction over me. Subconsciously, I thought Chao'an was in Chaoyang District of Beijing. So I asked them, "Is Chao'an a part from Chaoyang?" The interrogator was also surprised since I didn't know where the police came and arrested me. So he replied: "This is Chao'an County in Chaozhou of Guangdong Province." I said, "Chaozhou is not the right place to me! What do I have to do with Chaozhou?" So they told me that Yashily reported to the Chao'an police because of their suspicion of extortion. Therefore the police there have to accept their report and file the case accordingly. And another officer once threatened me by saying that "Guo, this is our control land of ChaoShan, you can't run away this time."

In fact, I didn't realize at the time that the business of

Yashily Scient Joint Venture was registered, operated in Guangzhou, the capital of Guangdong province. And they reported that the place where I committed the crime of extortion was in Beijing. No matter on what aspect you consider from a legal point of view, Chao'an County should not be the proper place for my case jurisdictions. The entire handling procedure of this case done by them was illegal and baseless. I just thought that the cross-provincial police were here to arrest me, as long as I cooperated with their cross-border investigation and explained or even defended against the case clearly, everything would be fine sooner or later.

It was absolutely impossible to tell the difference between day and night in the interrogation room. The investigators were divided into multiple teams and conducted dozens of rounds of continuous questioning on me without eating, drinking, going bathroom and sleeping. The content of the inquiry is about matters related to Yashily case. For examples, they asked me about my kid's entire medical inspection and breeding processes, where we bought the baby formula, and how long the kid had been feeding, what did we say to Yashily, what did we say to Scient Company, what did we say to the media, journalists, reporters and people around us, along with some other issues that had nothing to do with Yashily Int'l or Scient Company. The interrogation lasted for two days and two nights. During this period, they kept me compulsorily foot-and-hand-cuffed on the Chinese TIGER chair and did not allow me to eat, drink, use bathroom and sleep.

After the interrogation by the local Public Security Bureau, I was not released as I wished or expected, but was taken to the Chao'an County Detention Center. I was locked up alone in a small cell for one person only, which was about 1.5 square meters of size and 6 meters in height. There was only a plastic bucket for water and toilet container in the cell, as well as a plastic bowl and spoon sold by them to me at 50 yuan. My hands and feet were all chained, cuffed by the shackles weighing more than ten kilograms which was also fixed to the ground, making me impossible to move inside the cell. In addition, there is a video camera 3 meters above my head, and daily communication with outside between me and the center depends totally on this camera. Whenever I waved or yelled at the camera, someone would yell at me back from the

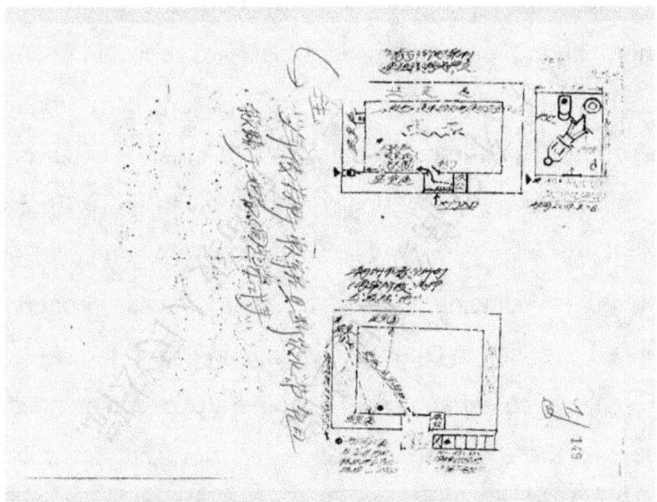

Drawing shows the small cell for one person only where Guo, Li
stayed in the Chao'an County Detention Center

loudspeaker and asked me what I wanted to do with them.

When arriving at the detention center, I realized that things were not as simple or imaginable as I thought. Thinking back to our negotiation process, my arrests across provinces from Hangzhou to Xiamen and then from Xiamen to Chao'an, if it was just a simple and legal investigation, it would not be like this at all. And it would not be such a BIG fight!

After I was detained in the detention center, the correctional officers and criminal suspects in the detention center verbally abused me, surrounded me and beat me, put me in restraints, denied me shopping, and restricted my food intake. These were all common occurrences they offered to me. My treatment in the center was extremely inhumane and tortured; I could only survive on moldy rice, soup without any fishy taste, and I was exploited by both the guards and prisoners during this endurable time. No sunlight, no real person inside the cells, and everything is beyond of my control. In the midst of extreme anxiety and loneliness, I could only cheer myself up every day, sing songs and even speak English to myself. For a long time, I was isolated or detained in solitary confinement, including before & after I was wrongfully sentenced to prison in Guangdong Jieyang Prison twice.

Even in such extremely cruel moment or circumstances, I still believe there will be a chance for me. After the retrial convenes, I will be acquitted by the court because I firmly believe that everything I did was 100% legal in China.

# Chapter 3.

## Guo was imprisoned, being tortured but refused to plead guilty, sentenced to five years behind bars

Because I insisted on not pleading guilty, in order to force me plead guilty and be convicted smoothly, I was held in solitary confinement in a small dark cell-room of the Chao'an County Detention Center for two weeks and then transferred to a "normal" prison. The prison cell was about 40 square meters and held more than 30 criminal suspects. Similar to what is shown in the crime dramas on TV, the local prison is actually managed by a government-appointed prisoners' chief. The police at the detention center should have informed the chief of prisoners in advance. According to the inmate rules of the center, I am a new prisoner, and the chief must provide me with a kind of "special care" and restraints. In the center, the chief forced me to do their work such as cleaning toilets. If I disobeyed or was slow on doing it, I would be physically insulted, food deducted or even brutally beaten by a group of jailbirds.

During prisoners' work break, I wanted to make some records or preparations for my trial case, and the limited pages of blank paper and ball-pen refills were strictly controlled by the center. During this period, like other prisoners, I was also forced to do labor work for the export-processing business, such as beading, making toys for kids and high-heeled shoes accessories for ladies. Since I refused them, I had been strictly restricted from extra daily food, monthly shopping, and daily diet supplements. After leaving the detention center, I met an inmate who had been detained in the center for several years and told me: "Li, when we were in the detention center, we

Main gate of Chao'an County Detention Center

could easily buy the letter paper, refills and use them. But one day all of a sudden, there are more than 20 people in our cell, except for the chief of prisoners, no one else is allowed to use those paper and refills anymore. I think this updated rule may be caused by you, you are really influential. "

In the detention center, prisoners still communicate with each other privately. For some unknown reason, some of them including the chief, always say to me from time to time: "Guo, forget it, you'd better plead guilty as soon as possible, otherwise you will suffer a lot from the consequence." During the interrogation process, the police officers from the Criminal Investigation Brigade, and prosecutors from the Procuratorate Dept. also threatened and lured me from time to time, saying: "Guo, we definitely didn't arrest you wrongly, you'd better admit it and plead the guilty", or "Be smart and fight for a better result! Have a good attitude and get a minor sentence, and better go home with a reduced sentence." However I firmly believe that I have nothing wrong. As parents, we feel guilty and worried that our kid has eaten a faked baby formula. As a consumer, the responsibility does not lie with my family at all. The ones who are at fault should be Yashily & Scient, the dairy companies that faked and produced it.

On November 20th 2009, the Chao'an County People's Court held a trial on my "extortion" case. Due to the influence

Repeal letter written by Guo, Li when he was in prison

of the "melamine" incident of China, my trial immediately triggered an uproar in public opinion. They strongly questioned why a case involving a harmed consumer in Beijing was tried in the court of Chao'an County in Guangdong Province, instead of being trialed in Beijing or Guangzhou, where Scient Company is actually located? My kid consumed the baby formula, which is branded by Scient as the US one. Yashily is only the controlling shareholder of the Scient JV in Guangzhou. Scient Guangzhou Company and Yashily Int'l Group are two independent operated companies, so why wasn't the case handled there in Guangzhou, where Scient is located with which we have been negotiating compensation issues? Instead, it was chosen to be processed and tried in a small county, where it is very very far away from Guangdong and Beijing?

In fact, the entire investigation and trial process of this case was illegal and unlawful. The main reason is known to all that Chao'an County of Guangdong is the hometown of Zhang Litian, a member of NPC and the boss of Yashily International. So they believe they can control all judicial resources around there; and since Guangzhou is a first-tier city in China, the corresponding judicial departments such as public security, procurator, courts, and prisons should handle cases in a relatively transparent and perhaps much "fair" manner; Guangzhou will not be as dark as Chao'an County, which directly resorts to illegal means such as using torture to coerce a statement. In court, when faced with the audio recordings produced by Yashily& Scient and the written materials with my past signatures of the claims, I felt extremely angry, but could not effectively defend myself. It seemed that the matter of case itself was just like it is, and my rights defending process just went with the flow. Yes, there was no doubt about that.

The plaintiff Yashily & Scient repeatedly approached me to negotiate compensation issues, and repeatedly induced me to modify the conditions and requirements, asking me to write the content as more specific and detailed as possible. Throughout the entire process of the case, they were deliberately concocting the appearance that we, as a victim family, kept asking for higher prices and went further and continued to claim compensation from them without a proper reason. It was only during the trial that I fully understood that Yashily & Scient did not really want to negotiate compensation with us. This is a trap designed by them! The purpose of setting such a trap is to prevent me from continuing to defend my family's rights and expose the scandal to the media, so as not to affect Yashily's going public process in Hong Kong.

From the time I was arrested to the first trial on the court, it lasted just over three months. Based on the complexity and amount of money involved in the case of "extortion" I was accused of, the background of the victim's company Yashily & Scient, and the attention paid by the media or other factors, the speed of my trial to close this case can be described as the speed of light with reference to other similar criminal cases.

Presumably, the Guangdong Yashily Group and Scient US Company at that time wanted to resolve my case quickest possible in order to subside the public opinion and prevent the possible abortion of their plot for going public in Hong Kong!

On January 8th 2010, Chao'an County Court of Guangdong Province held that the means adopted by the defendant Guo, Li on reporting to the media will directly distort the reality of the efforts of Yashily Int'l Group and Scient Guangzhou to create their market credit, and will be enough to damage the reputation of the twos, and affects the normal operations of the businesses and arouses fear in the two companies. Therefore, it should be determined that Guo objectively committed an act of coercion in the sense of Chinese criminal law.

The Court also used the recording of negotiation between the parts and the testimony of my ex-wife Gao Hong and her close friend) called ZhangLin as the main case evidence or witnesses. In the first instance, I was found guilty of extortion and sentenced to five years in Chinese prison.

Before the verdict came out, I was prepared for the worst, but I still didn't expect that the Chao'an Court would give such an arbitrary verdict. I refused to accept it and firmly appealed. On February 5th 2010, a few days right after a week of my appeal, my first-instance court defense lawyer Gong Sunxue tried to ask the Chaozhou Intermediate Court that Guo Li's appeal was about to be filed in the court of his second-instance procedure. However, the Chaozhou Intermediate Court did not notify my family or the lawyer of this. And the second instance ruling was issued almost at the same time to my end with a result of: the original judgment was upheld. It means that my appeal process was deprived and ended hastily without even taking the required time and legal process.

"Guo Li had neither the intention to illegally possess nor the means to actually carry out threats or coercion. His claim was based on the infringement behavior of Scient JV Company and the offer behavior of Scient & Yashily Group, which has a strong legal basis. Therefore, his crime of extortion cannot be established." My defense lawyer said this in an interview that she believed that the Chaozhou Intermediate Court did not even "have time" to look at the case files and made a hasty judgment, which was a clear sign of guilty conscience.

The jailbirds and other prisoners at the detention center advised me after I passed the first-instance verdict: "Guo, it's better not to appeal. It's useless and just a waste of your time." After my original sentence was quickly upheld in the second trial, they came to persuade me again: "Guo, stop tossing about it, go to jail as soon as possible. Just go to prison, plead guilty and accept the court punishment. If you behave well in jail, your sentence will be reduced. In this way, one and a half years will be reduced from your five-year sentence." "In three more years, you can get out of the prison."

There is no other way. I think that only by persisting in not pleading guilty for my five years imprisonment can I have the opportunity to appeal and be vindicated. So I asked my former lawyer to tell my family, and when my family members visited me in Jieyang prison of Guangdong, that they must write a letter of accusation and complaint to the relevant departments every month to make the complaint and accusation for me.

In this way, an unjust case was settled. Even if there is a dispute between me and Yashily Scient Companies, it is still a civil case. Now, not only have a civil case been turned into a criminal one, but right and wrong have also been reversed, and the cart before the horse has been turned, turning a real victim into an aggressor. Faced with such a result, I could not accept it and could only silently persist in the future struggle in prison. Right after February 2010, the Chinese lunar new year, I was taken to Jieyang Prison from Chaozhou in Guangdong Province and began serving my sentence.

The only way left is to appeal. At the same time, Gong Sunxue, the former first-instance lawyer, disclosed the details of my case to the outside world and the media.

After being sent to Jieyang Prison in Guangdong Province, I was first sent to the intensive training section for a month of their comprehensive training. The prison section is five stories high, with two to five floors, each floor has 5-6 cells, and each cell accommodates at least 14 prisoners. Because I did not plead guilty, the prison guards in the section, the chief in the cell, and CCP activists among the criminals targeted me with physical harm, corporal punishment, and deprivation of meals and other strict torture measures throughout the month. For example: I was not allowed to go to the bathroom normally, was only allowed 3-4 hours of sleep every night. The "Chinese Prison Law" stipulates that prisoners should go to bed at 21 o'clock, but I was often punished by them until 2 to 3 o'clock in

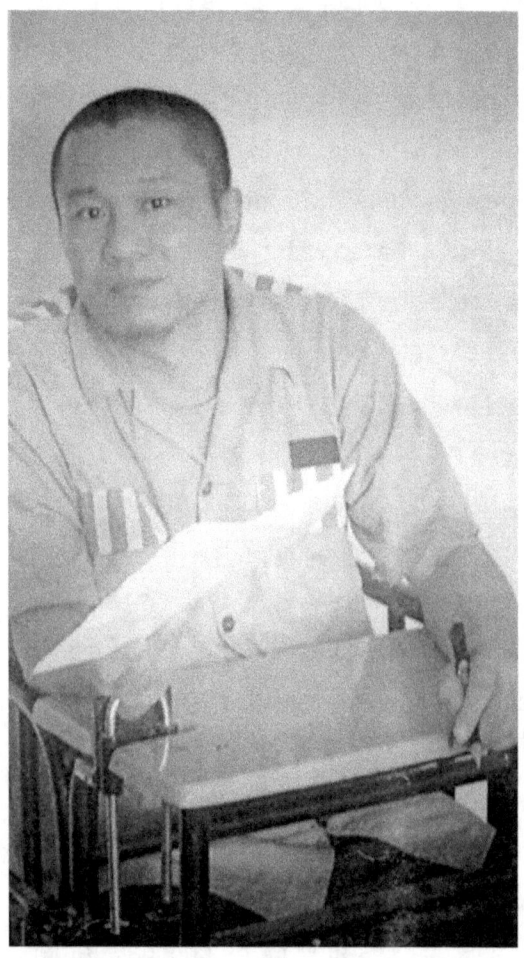

The Torture Chair used to force Guo, Li to sit in Chinese prisons,

also being called the Tiger Stool

the early morning.

During outdoor training exercises, the prison guards often turned their backs to other prisoners and used verbal threats, physical punishment and humiliation on me in uninhabited corners. They also used police equipment such as "WanFu" (an extremely high voltage like 10KV) electric batons to perform so-called corrections on me. In the name of the law, they used starvation therapy and beatings to teach me a lesson. Another example: During the training, they forced me to stand in a fixed position for a long time in an attempt to force me to plead guilty and commit suicide. During this period, the prison guards also kicked my injured body with leather shoes and asked me to stay in a squatting position for more than half an hour. If I stayed slow or refused to obey squat, they would punish me with electric batons. In the cell, the prison guards instructed the chief to educate me by reading the rules of prison and punish me corporally. If I didn't cooperate, I would be deprived of sleep, shower, and meals. At the same time, they would verbally abuse me, force me to recite prison rules, and insult my personality. The purpose of this method is to force me to give up my belief, plead guilty and obey their "GuiJu" or rules (A proof that Guo, Li did not participate in labor reform work in jails, did not receive rewards, and did not receive meals supply incentive).

I was sentenced to five years in both trials. While serving my sentence in prison, I never thought or believed that I was

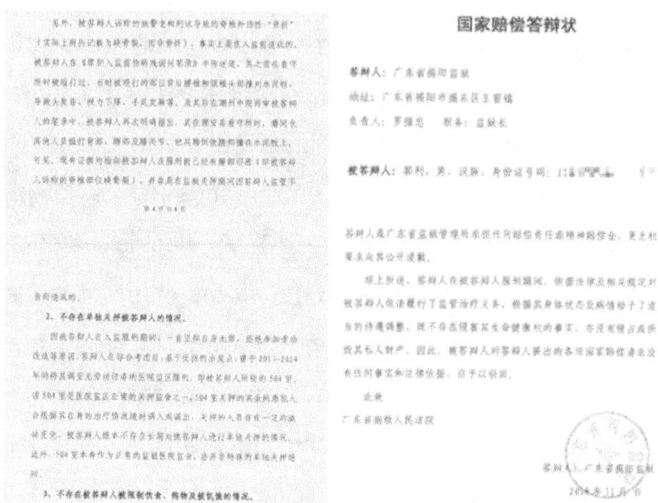

Documents about repealing and National Compensation

guilty and firmly resisted their reforms and pleaded not guilty. On May 31st 2010, it seemed that the case had taken another major turn. The Guangdong Provincial High Court issued the No. 1 retrial decision, saying that the procedures in my case are illegal. The Chaozhou intermediate court of my original court of second instance was ordered to retry the case.

After nearly five months of waiting, the judges and bailiffs from the Chaozhou Intermediate Court took me to the Chaozhou Detention Center to await the first retrial. When a retrial occurs due to major flaws in a case, the court usually sends personnel to Jieyang prison to conduct the trial. After hearing that I was going back to the detention center (not remain to stay in Jieyang prison) for retrial, all the prisoners including the ones who were currently serving their sentence in prison agreed that my verdict would definitely be changed to not guilty in this retrial!

This is how the law stipulates that prisoners should leave with their own spending money accounts. However, when the police from the Prison Affairs Department of Guangdong Jieyang Prison went through the procedures for me to be transferred to the Chaozhou Public Security Detention Center, they said: "Guo, Li, we won't give you this time your account transferred to the center, because you will definitely be sent back." At that time, I was thinking: How do you know whether I can come back or not? It is not the Jieyang Prison that has the final say, but the law and court. For this reason I remain determined! I was thinking...the "unusual" move of taking me back to the public security detention center during the retrial must be to let me out and free. But later the facts proved that this was a "judicial public performance", performed for the public. Guo Li was found guilty in accordance with the law through "courts of first and second instance", which not only

The main gate of Jieyang Prison

calmed the media's enthusiasm, diverted the public's attention, but also bought enough time and cleared obstacles for Yashily to go public in Hong Kong.

Similarly, Jieyang Prison hopes to use long-term abuse, beating and torture to force me to compromise or plead guilty. This will better prove that Guo, Li is guilty in this concocted "extortion" case, and he has already pleaded guilty and served the law. Therefore, during three month time after I was retried

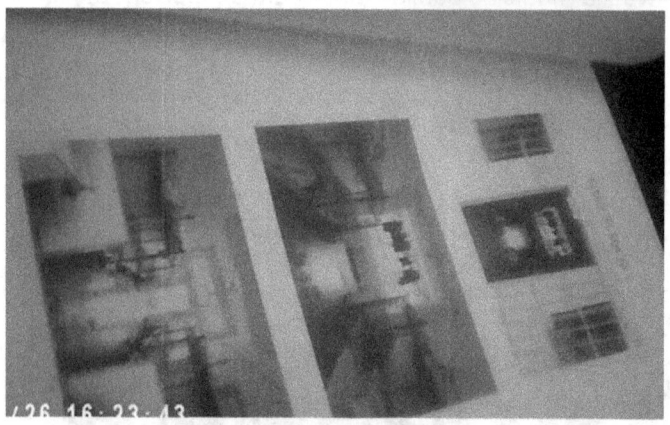

The two solitary confinement cells of Jieyang Prison

where Guo, Li stayed in for long time

and sent back to the public security detention center, Guangdong Jieyang Prison under the Ministry of Justice deliberately froze and withheld the account of my living expenses in the prison. This resulted in me having no money to spend in the Guangdong Chaozhou Detention Center under the Ministry of Public Security, unable to purchase my daily groceries inside the jail, resulting in my sufferings of hunger and malnutrition. In the final analysis, they wanted to force me to surrender in this way and compel me to submit.

In the retrial of Chaozhou Intermediate Court, in fact, internally, the tone has undoubtedly been set for Guo Li to maintain his original verdict. Around the Chinese spring festival of 2011, Jieyang Prison saw that I had always refused to plead guilty and to submit, so they invited my parents to visit the prison and asked them to try to persuade me for the last chance.

That meeting is still fresh and profound in my memory. In fact, I haven't seen my relatives for nearly a year, and my parents were very excited when they saw me through the thick window. Shortly after the interview, my mother persuaded me that the management of Jieyang Prison had said that as long as I confessed my crime, my sentence would be commuted. After the sentence was reduced, I would be able to be freed easily in just over a year or so. At this time, the police officers from Prison Affairs Section were just standing behind them. They went on to say: If you still refuse to plead guilty, the prison has told them that you will be severely punished. When I heard my mother persuade me to surrender, I immediately felt angry and started to shout loudly: "It is impossible for me to surrender and plead guilty." During the past year I was jailed in the detention center, no one could really help me and no one can understand the inhuman torture I suffered. Even my parents were being taken advantage of especially by the prison as lobbyist, which made me extremely disappointed. The belief of innocence has always supported me during the five years of my sentence. Even if I continued to plead innocence after I was released from prison, I had long been mentally prepared to be killed in Jieyang prison.

When I was interrogated by the judge of Chaozhou Intermediate Court, I made an application saying that if I were found guilty again in the retrial, I asked the court not to send me back to Jieyang Prison to serve my sentence anymore. I

Bosses of Yashily celebrating their stock got listed in Hong Kong

have stated in my transcripts many times that I was mistreated by other prisoners and guards in a collective and organized way at Jieyang Prison. If I were sent back to Jieyang Prison again, I might not be able to get out of it. I also proposed that even if I were sent to a remote region called Xinjiang to serve my rest sentence, I would prefer not to be sent back to Jieyang Prison AGAIN!

All prisoners who have served their sentences know that the environment in prison is much better than that in a detention center. In addition to have a better living conditions and larger space for activities, there are also working meals and food supply incentives, and a better shopping and living conditions. And the most important thing is that in prison, if criminals "behave well", they can get reduced sentences and even parole rewards. But I know that these "preferential treatment" actually have nothing to do with me. To me, to be honest, Jieyang Prison is just hell on earth.

A case was finally tried and retried in the same court, which is unique in the history of modern consumer rights defending events in China. In the first retrial on December 30th of the same year, Chaozhou Intermediate Court determined that the past trial procedures were not illegal and that the two judgments of my case were not improper. The retrial upheld the original judgment. This ruling was equivalent to the lower court overturning the facts and evidence determined by the higher one, and given a loud slap in the face to the high court.

And the slightest hope for justice through a retrial was fleeting.

For this reason, I had to be sent back to Jieyang Prison by the Chaozhou Public Security No. 1 Detention Center. Chaozhou Intermediate Court ignored my written request not to send me back to Jieyang Prison. Being held alone with strict isolation measure in its prison, I no longer knew the progress of this case or whether it would receive more media attention. As for filing a complaint and an appeal, my family members living far away in Beijing can only be relied on helping me.

Interestingly, when I was escorted back to Jieyang Prison to go through the procedures for my re-incarceration, the 893 yuan in my personal spending money account that my parents in Beijing had remitted through the China Post to the Chaozhou detention center was also misappropriated by my court judge JIANG Hai and a team of bailiffs on my way back to the prison. Because prisoners are not allowed to keep cash personally while in their custody. After I left the detention center to check out and sign the bill, the Chaozhou Public Security Detention Center handed the cash to the above-mentioned escorting judge JIANG and his team in person. I discovered this money after I was released from prison in July 2014 that they did not transfer it to my account in Jieyang Prison as the stipulations required, but taken and kept it privately. In subsequent claims of my "State Compensation Package" case, the court personnel involved in the scandal was also reduced in rank from a senior judge to a file clerk in office. I think the punishment is well deserved.

The guards and most prisoners in Jieyang Prison all speak "ChaoShan" dialect. Although I know some foreign language, I can't understand it at all. In order to suppress and subjugate me, they were very cooperative and never spoke Mandarin in front of me. After cooperating with the prison police to use both "hard and soft" violence to make me surrender for several months, they kept me in solitary confinement on the 5th floor of their special single-ward in the prison hospital for a long time. I was unable to see the sun from inside the ward and had been keeping in a tortured, malnourished condition. This caused me to suffer from diabetes, peripheral nerve damage, spine injury, numbness in limbs, bronchitis, stomach problems, memory loss and trance-like illnesses. Because I persisted in not pleading guilty, I refused to participate in their reform-through-labor work inside the prison manufacturing facilities, resulting in no work-record of my labor reform. The prison

Drawing on flowers by Guo, Li when he was in prison

management did not allow me for extra meals they offered to other prisoners, restricted my purchase of necessary non-staple food for my daily feeding. In the end, I could only buy some basics like pre-made or high-sugar sweets and cookies to temporarily satisfy my hunger or relieve my long-term starvation.

When I first entered Jieyang prison, almost all prisoners and police officers would think that I was a liar, pretending to be crazy and stupid. No one believed that a former white-collar or nick-named "No-Collar-Man" who spoke good English and worked for the embassies in the Chinese capital Beijing would be "parachuted" to the ChaoShan region and sentenced to prison, where it was a place "a bird doesn't even poop".

Life in prison is really hard! Many times I don't even know if I am still alive. Even if the prisoners are alive, in a cruel

Drawing on turtle by Guo, Li when he was in prison

environment with high walls and electric grid, they just look like walking corpses. In order to relieve my anger in my mind and overcome the loneliness, to alleviate the mental and physical pain or brutality I suffered when I was beaten, tortured and starved by them, to be able to go out and continue to appeal after my five year jail term, and to avoid the possible loss of speech caused by dominating solitary confinement, I have always firmly believed in my heart: keep practicing calligraphy, reading aloud and learning foreign languages.

The stagnant environment of Jieyang prison was broken. They were all shocked, and "TongGai" or inmates thought I was talking crazy. In order to prove something, the prison management invited their staff and some their trusted prisoners who "know English" to come check and listen secretly. After checking or listening, they began to believe that Guo, Li was indeed a legendary character of (simultaneous interpreter) translator. After being released from prison in 2016, an inmate named ZHANG Zhitie who lives in Wuqing of Tianjin, recalled in an interview with Beijing Television Studio: "Guo was so out of place in Jieyang prison. He didn't have the slightest attitude of "pleading guilty and obeying the law". He had the courage to not be afraid of being tortured to death. The prison was totally isolated from the outside world. Yes, we will all feel scared due to it like a hell environment and cannot bear the stress and pressure of it. Only Guo is not afraid of anything inside the prison, and he firmly believes that he is the right one."

Once, my parents and brother came to visit me in Jieyang prison together. The visit usually lasted only half an hour or so. My brother said to me: "Brother, we want to find someone for you to smoothen "GuanXi" (a special connection) and help you come out as soon as possible." When I heard this, I went crazy and waved my fists up and down and shouted at them: "It is impossible for me to surrender, and I will never surrender to THEM!" My mother later said in an interview that it was the most excited moment of me she's ever seen in her life.

After they returned to Beijing, my parents tried to write a letter of appeal on the computer. After this, my mother took out the saved one for printing them out with a multiple copies. Then she brought them back home and bound them one by one ready for mailing. There was a "Yellow Book of China National

Guo, Li and one of his friends

Ministries & Commissions" sold in the Yongdingmen Wai of Beijing. It cost seven yuan (~US$1.00 ) a copy, and my mother bought three copies in just one go. When she saw that my case could be reported to the relevant Chinese department, then she sent a letter of appeal there. Among them, the most frequent mailings are sent to the High Court of Guangdong Province, which was delivered once a month from Beijing. Every time before sending a letter of appeal, my parents have to revise it again and again. After having them mailed through the registered mail, the staff at China Post office in Beijing got to know my mother very well and further asked in a low voice: "Auntie Xin, are you somewhat in trouble NOW?"

During my five year sentence in prison, despite the long distance afar from Beijing, my mother never missed an opportunity to visit me. A mother knows her child very well. She only needs to look at my eyes, talk a few words, and through my body gestures to know clearly on what happened to me inside the prison. Gradually... my mother, who was 73 years old at the time, began to hate Guangdong. For example, she cannot listen to Cantonese songs and feels uncomfortable when she hears someone talk in Cantonese. After I was imprisoned, major TV stations across the country were still broadcasting prime-time commercials for Yashily and Scient baby formula. One of their spokespersons (including movie stars Jiang Wenli, Yao Chen etc.) was Pu Cunxin, a China national first-class actor, member of National Committee of

Chinese People's Political Consultative Conference, and dean of China People's Arts Academy. After watching it, my mother wrote to Pu asking: You are a famous "national face" actor in the country, why do you choose to advertise for a "China faked US Scient Baby Formula"? Later, for unknown reason, the live characters of Pu, and Jiang in these advertisements were replaced by the characters in animations. Only then did my mother stop writing letters to Pu.

Faced with the temptation of getting a reduced sentence and an early freedom by pleading guilty, the persuasion of my family, the inmates, and the opportunity to have extra meals in prison and the opportunity to buy canned meats to feed oneself by pleading guilty, my will of innocence has never been wavered. The parents were a little confused at first, and people around me thought: How could the three-level courts make the wrong decision? How could the police department make the wrong arrest? How could the procurator make the wrong prosecution again? Even if they make a mistake once, will they make a mistake repeatedly like the one you had? After multiple procedures of investigation, prosecution, first and second trials, and retrials by the police, prosecutors, and courts, people even began to doubt themselves. Is it true that I am trying to avoid reform through labor by "making strong arguments" or "abusing the resources of law"? For this reason, they all kept urging me to plead guilty quickly and try to get a reduced sentence and get out as soon as possible. But I insisted on my innocence, so why should I plead guilty? And I firmly believe that only by not doing that can I be worthy of myself and my harmed child.

Not long after I was imprisoned, in-between the 2nd trial and 1st retrial, I received a divorce request from my wife GaoHong. I know that in such situation, it is quite common for a couple to file for divorce, so I am not surprised. Two judges from Haidian Court in Beijing came to Jieyang Prison in Guangdong Province to seek my signature and opinion. They believed that I was unable to take care of my minor child while serving my sentence in jail, and supported that the other part who filed for divorce should have custody and support. I suggested that because my wife suffers from severe depression, she needs sufficient financial resources to take care of our child. GaoHong cannot be independent on her own, and a reliable supervisor

Drawing of Guo, Li and his daughter by himself when he was in prison

should be added. After discussions between the court and our family, Haidian Court ordered that my child's grandmother, TaoXin, be the actual dependent. We got divorced and I lost custody of my child right after this. In those dark days when I

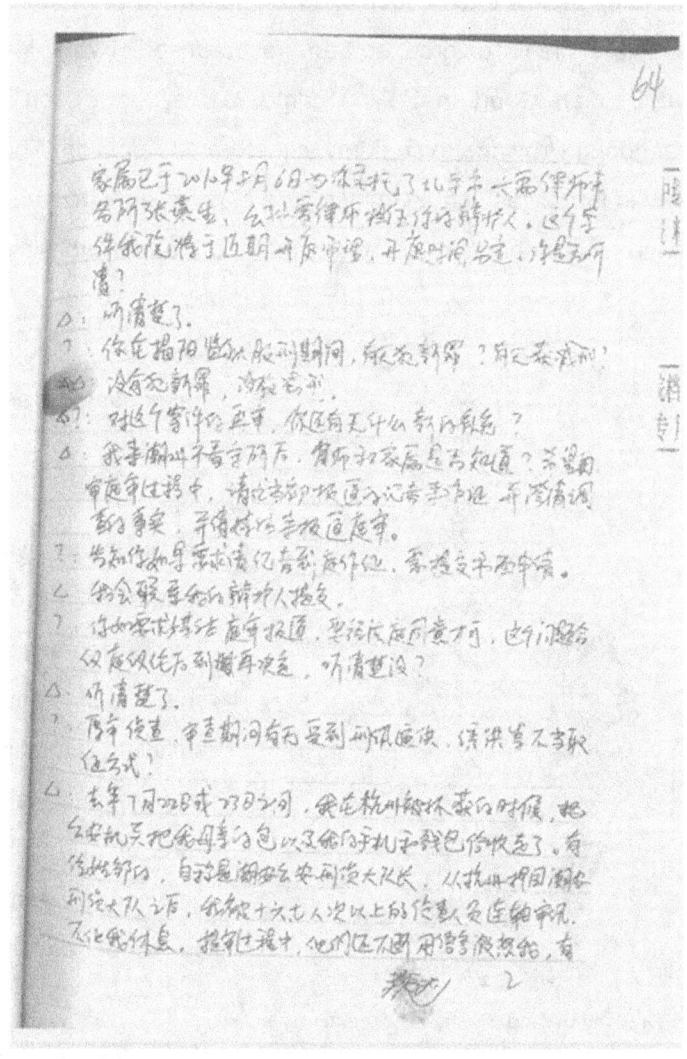

One page of Records on Court's Questions and Answers

was totally isolated from the outside world, I gradually forgot the appearance of my sweet child Yiyi. Whenever I think of taking her to play on the water of West Lake in Hangzhou, Zhejiang province before she was three years old, I think of pushing her in a stroller on the ramp of the Xizhimen Flyover in Beijing. The stroller made a rattling sound when it went down

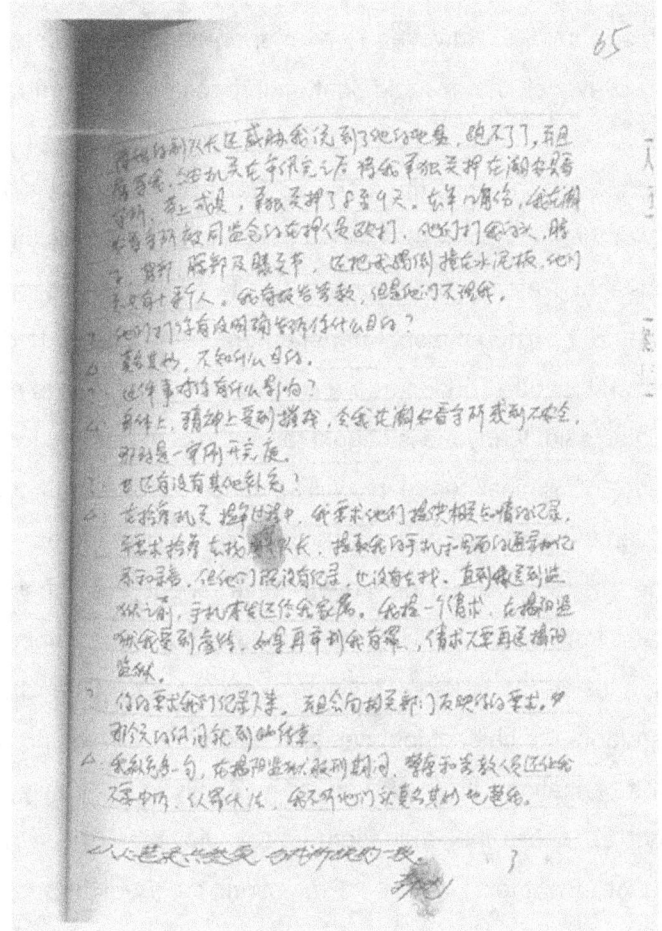

Another page of Records on Court's Questions and Answers

the ramp, and the child sitting inside the stroller laughed and laughed... For this, I picked up a pen and drew in my thoughts a picture of her.    Actually I couldn't remember her appearance, so I tried to draw her back only.

From a bright and respectable man to a prisoner, my family was gone, and I was truly separated from my wife and child. I never thought that I would ever experience something like this in my life. However, I never seemed to be defeated, and I always felt that I would fight until reaching to the end of tunnel.

In the prison, I was the major subject of strict supervision and was often changed to different sections of prison for their forced-labor reform or switched to be held in solitary confinement. The prison management and the guards stipulated that other prisoners were not allowed to speak to me. They also said: If anyone is caught talking to Guo, the reduced sentence of criminal treatments will be cancelled or suspended, and even the sentence of the caught criminal will be increased by the management. Don't even think about them being released from prison early. I remember that during a "training" session inside the strict supervision section or "YanGuanDui" in Mandarin, the chief of inmates also asked me to use part of my compensation I had received from Yashily to my family in Beijing to bribe the management of Jieyang Prison in exchange for the "Umbrella Protection" or BaoHuSan in Mandarin and "GuanXi" treatment of my life in prison. Options such as the "facilitating" role provided for individual commutation were also rejected by me.

When I was released from prison after serving my sentence and appealed for acquittal, several former inmates also said similar things in interviews with reporters: They said that I was like air in prison and no one dared to get along with me. Even if they have some contact with me after they are released from prison, they will be harassed, tracked and warned by "GuoBao" (secret police agent) and community services from all over the country. In one word: they are not allowed to have any contact with me. I asked them if they were given any tasks by GuoBao (Special Police)? In my subsequent "State Compensation" case application, I also mentioned that I was held in "solitary" custody in Jieyang prison. But the responsible authorities for compensation said back: While serving his sentence in prison, Guo was unsociable and unwilling to communicate with others.

Due to long-term starvation, beatings, corporal punishment and solitary confinement, the prison's severe punishment for "not pleading guilty and disobeying the law" caused me to suffer from multiple chronic diseases and permanent sequelae of trauma. As a result of it, my body was accompanied by peripheral nerve damage, spasms, cramping and memory decline problem and diseases. Because I was worried that severe memory loss and long-term occlusion would lead to speech aphasia or loss of basic communication skills, therefore I always insisted on learning to draw and write in prison, associated with reading, singing and talking to myself.

I remember that right after the year 2011, in order to understand how my language proficiency was "maintained" in jail at that time, I "took the opportunity to sign up" to take the exams of four selected courses for the "Self-study Examination for Higher Education in Prison" of Guangdong. When the results came out, only two subjects barely passed the scores of 60, and one only scored 20 (the total score of each subject was 100). Before being imprisoned, I was one of the top international simultaneous interpreters in China. With such a poor score, one can imagine how serious my health problem and memory impairment were. However, the situation in which I took the exam was described by Jieyang Prison in Guangdong as a sign of "in good health condition" during the

Guo, Li with his inmate friends outside the jail

claims, cross-examination sessions in the case of judicial infringement and "Guo, Li State Compensation" case after my wrongful case was reversed since 2017.

Speaking of organizing "prisoners who are close to the CCP government or GuanXi" to take the national higher education self-study examination, during the process of taking the above-mentioned examination in Jieyang Prison, I found that local education department and the prison system were using the examination results to be included in the rewards of their commutation and parole process. The rewards and performance used to request the court to commute the sentences of reference prisoners have actually formed a

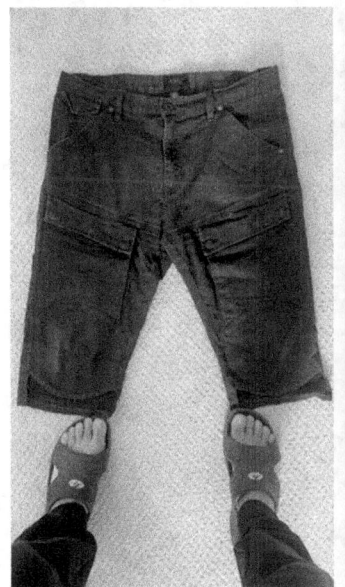

Products made from Chinese prison, verified by Li Guo, bought from
Winners in Ottawa, Canada, 2022

complete "trading" platform for public bribery. And it was actually an open trading triangle among criminals, prison, and court. During its 90 minutes of the exam, the prison officials and outside invigilators shut down their live video monitor in the middle of the exam in order to "cooperate" with the "DaJiao" prisoners' cheating on exams. After they copied the correct answers to the questions provided by the Education Dept. of Higher Learning in advance, before collecting the finished papers, the prison officials turn on the video monitor for invigilation again. It will be perfect for all and everyone in "the triangle" fraud will be happy!

The truck carrying cargos produced in Jieyang Prison

After a prisoner passes the examination, he may receive an additional commutation of sentence for at least half a year based on his performance. This is a "super-national" treatment in prison! This type of prisoner takes exams, tries to get a college diploma, which is a hot spot for publicity of Chinese prison reform system. Many of these candidates have not graduated from elementary school or junior high school. The question is, under the conditions of rehabilitation with extremely heavy work labor in prison, as prisoners, what ability and time do they have to directly take the college examination through self-study and obtain such good SCORE results? During this period, they bribed the education and police officers through the prisoners' families. What they saw was that the prisoners who have "GuanXi" obtained diplomas and received additional reduced sentences and rewards from fraud and corruption. The education department and officials inside and outside the prison received bribes and benefits through the education. The prison system under the Ministry of Justice has also established a good management image and social effect, which is simply the best of all for "triangle" relationship. In another word: Killing THREE birds with ONE stone.

In order to force me to participate in labor reform, Jieyang Prison tried every means and method to try to make it possible. Because of being harmed and injured, when I was in physical training several times, the police officers arranged for other disabled prisoners to surround me for drills and demonstrations, in order to influence my mind, they used both influence and analogy, threaten me to obey them. When they asked me stand up and squat down, other prisoners simply fell down beside me one by one after the police officer gave them an order. None of this could shake my attitude of not admitting guilt and my determination to stand firm and fight. When I was forced to participate in labor work in the manufacturing facilities, because I could not walk normal, Jieyang prison and the section I stayed using a hand trolley to commute me daily between the dorms and workshop, where they made export garments and packaging product there. My trolley was pushed by some activists at the front of the team every time, going back and forth between the dormitory and the workshop, followed by hundreds of prisoners. However when I arrived at the production facilities, I resolutely resisted in accordance with the law and refused to work on it. I did not accept their labor reform on me at all.

During this period, when other prisoners saw me like this, they also imitated me and began to slack off in their work, or even stopped working on strike. Because my resistance has seriously affected the mind, enthusiasm for labor reform and work efficiency of other prisoners in Jieyang Prison. Finally, Jieyang Prison moved me to several different sections and workshops, including changing my job type. For example, they changed my sewing job from making garments for exporting to North America to an electronic accessories workshop assembling Apple and Huawei data cables.

However I still don't accept it. In the end, they tried to send me to a teaching & research group to write reports for prison management or police guards, or keep record of conversations with prisoners about their "XiNao" (or Brainwash) and ideology reform, and to be responsible for "easy and comfortable" tasks such as doing laundry services for the police. Doing jobs as prisoners like these "DaJiaos" (BigFeet in English) you have to spend a lot of money to get "GuanXi" (special connections) from them. However they were also all refused and rejected by me. I fought in various forms in Jieyang prison, which allowed me to survive until the last day I was released from there in July 2014.

Prisoner is working as cheap labor

Chapter 4.

After being wrongfully imprisoned,
released after serving a full sentence,
Guo got prepared to appeal

On July 22nd 2014, five years imprisonment to me, not a single day missing! I served five years in prison and was released in accordance with the Chinese prison law. On the day I walked out of Jieyang prison gate, after inspection by the prison administration, I vowed to come out with two boxes of books that have accompanied me for the last one year in jail. I didn't know the man waiting for me in the minivan outside until he told me that during the last five years I was in prison, because my family went to Jieyang prison to visit me and helped me appeal in Beijing, they met this man in the Chaoshan area and asked him to errands for us locally. Since he was not a family member, he could not meet with me in jail in advance. Therefore, no one knew when I would walk out of the prison and gain my physical freedom that day, so I had to wait outside and next to the prison wall. In several hours after I walked out of the prison alone, a local minivan took me to the town center for a street food, and then the man sent me to the newly completed ChaoShanJie Airport to meet my family and return to Beijing.

My brother met me at the airport and helped me change out of my clothes from the prison. After five years imprisonment, I have completely lost touch with society. My expression at this moment was like a fool, unable to do anything. When I arrived at the ChaoShanJie airport, my brother helped me check in my luggage of books, change my boarding pass, and gave me a temporary mobile phone. He helped me call my mother who lives in Beijing. At that time, I just wanted to tell her that I'm out and still alive.

Coming back to the world of sunshine from a hell on earth where it was full of darkness, narrowness, filth and fear, I suddenly felt overwhelmed. However, the breath of freedom exuding in the fresh air, the relaxation and joy when my body and soul are released, make me think a lot and my heart surging. Because I hadn't seen so many people in a long time, and I was held in solitary confinement for a long time without being able to see the sun. For a short period of time, my breathing and vision became extremely labored, my thinking was very confused, and I felt at a loss what to do. I haven't had a full meal with fresh vegetables and meats in a long time, and I don't know what the aroma of the food will be like! In prison, I longed for delicious food, but when I was released from prison, I lost the desire that humans should have. I don't understand prices or how to spend money. When I go out to buy something, I will give someone two or three hundred yuan (US$30.00~50.00) for something worth tens of yuan (US$~5.00), but I don't know if I will ask for change. I have been out for quite some time and when I need to use the computer, I have forgotten all the passwords on how to start the computer and save it. Seeing me at a loss and thinking like a disabled man, my father didn't want to believe it and thought I was pretending to it. He once said: "You were faking it in prison, why are you still faking it when you get out of it!" When I think of this at that time and even to today, I can not help

News report of Guo, Li on AFR Financial Review

crying at this scene...

After settling in, I immediately went to find my Yiyi, the child I hadn't seen for five years, whom I thought about day and night. As soon as she saw me, she blurted out "Daddy", which made me feel relieved and happy. She called me to show that she has not forgotten me. My child also said that I looked like an alien who had returned from another planet. To this purpose, she also drew a picture, which showed a man with two wings flying from the sky, and on the ground was a little girl, waiting for her father to fly back. When I asked why he had a pair of wings, she added that because daddy flew back from another planet.

The first time I met my kid, her grandmother TaoXin brought her to my end. I was very touched at the time and didn't know how to explain it to them; why had her daddy disappeared for five years? My kid was 8 years old at that time and was still ignorant. She showed some timidity when she met me. With my sudden appearance and the charges I was carrying, how could I explain or express to her that as a father, I had been wrongly accused by judicial abuses... I couldn't help

Originally drew by Yiyi, Guo, Li's daughter, on a white board

but secretly make up my mind. During the five years in prison, I never changed my mind about never compromising or admitting guilt. Now for the sake of my kid, myself and my family, I must clear my grievances and act immediately to prove my innocence. After that, I couldn't wait to collect evidence and prepare for the appeal and complaint.

The second time I met my kid, I remember going to school to pick her up from there. Her grandmother made a bet with me, saying that I had not lived with the child for more than five years, and we would see if I could take her back to our No.412 condo in Xizhimen of Beijing. My condo is in the direction to the left after leaving her school, while her grandma's is not far from the school and to the right. After I picked up the kid alone, the kid who was holding hands with me didn't even look back and just walked to the left direction. At this time, her grandmother followed us for nearly a hundred meters, stumbling to catch up, grabbed the child's hand and pulled her back immediately. She didn't expect her granddaughter to leave with me so easily. I still remember the panic in her grandma's eyes at that time and I couldn't bear it! So far, I have had many thoughts on the issue of seeking "custody of the child" that I had previously fought for, and I have done many ideological struggles and psychological constructions. Under constant reminders of this situation, I tended to give up on regaining it. The reason is: Since I have served five years in prison, my kid and her grandmother's family have established a very deep-in-blood relationship and connection. I JUST don't want to hurt them. We JUST take this as a boundary!

Because I have been out of touch with society for years, many of my words and deeds appear to be different and out of place in the eyes of outsiders and my family members. Usually acting just like a fool! My father and brother even thought I was faking the symptoms. They used to tell me: Li, you played dumb inside the jail, why are you still playing when you come out of it? My mother felt very sorry for me and always felt that I had suffered five years of tortures and unjust. After I was released from Jieyang prison, I should start a new life, find a new job, have a family, and maybe have another baby. No one around me supported a continuation to appeal or complaint. Almost everyone advised me just forget it, stop fight or you can't succeed.... Because I was quite anxious, eager to overturn the verdict, and eager to regain my past job and skills, some of my movements were deformed and had no edge. In many times, I would appear particularly depressed. After I came back, I had no source of income. My brother didn't dare to have contact with me because of his job nature in mainland China. He could only secretly give my mother one to two thousand yuan (USD140.00~280.00) every month, plus some money my mother saved from her pension to me in another one thousand yuan (USD140.00). This is all my monthly income or spending money. Despite this limitation, I still never thought about backing down. I must appeal and reverse the wrong case. When I go out to do errands, I try to save as much money as possible and plan frugally. I prefer to take the cheapest and slowest transportation in the country, eat the cheapest food boxes, and stay in the cheapest budget hotels. I feel like I am back overnight to the life in the 1980s of China.

Just a few months after I came out from the jail, I lived with my parents for some reasons. Because my father could not understand and support my daily "jailed" habits and my continued fight to defend my legal rights, we had several conflicts during this period. After that, I had no choice but to move out and return to my own No.412 condo where I lived years before. In the condo, I found that many case evidence materials and personal belongings, including baby formula samples and original quality inspection reports, and some valuables such as Australia aboriginal's stamp collection and Lamborghini racing suits were also missing. In addition, on July 23rd 2009 when I was arrested in Hangzhou of Zhejiang province on the same day, the Guangdong Provincial Public Security Dept. illegally seized my Beijing property across provinces. Later in 2019, I filed a complaint and claim for compensation against Chaozhou Public Security Bureau, Guangdong Provincial Public Security Dept. and Guangdong Provincial Jieyang Prison in accordance with the "State Compensation Law" to hold them accountable.

Although five years have passed, the public's concern about melamine and food safety has not diminished just because I was convicted by the Guangdong Provincial

Judiciary, and the public does not think that I was guilty or wrong after being sentenced. A few years after I was released from Jieyang prison, the media continued to pay a continued attention to me and my further fight. Several mainstream media continued to interview and report on me, such as infzm.com, Radio Free Asia, Voice of America and IAFK Canada, etc..

Because the appeal requires further evidence collection and case analysis, my relevant case files are actually in the hands of the lawyers from Beijing Dayu Law Firm who was my original first-instance agent. After being released from prison, I found lawyer Yansheng & Gongsun and they met me for this, I used to have high expectations on them. Although the second trial and first retrial of my case were intervened by the Ministry of Justice (Yashily Dairy's protecting umbrella, former Minister

Wu, Aiying, Former Minister of Justice, PRC

of Justice Wu Aiying) in China, it was virtually impossible to hire a "normal" lawyer in China for me. So I have to defend the case myself. Because at the first trial, my lawyers said in their defense paper that my rights defending behavior was not extortion; then I think the lawyers and I have the same view on this, and my case is a false extortion, fabricated by Yashily Int'l with the Chinese local judiciary.

But after the meeting, my original first-instance lawyer just hit me in the head, and my idea was all wishful thinking. By hearing my strongest desire of appeal, they said that although my idea was correct and feasible, however as they are lawyers and a law firm, it is not a "charity" issue. After all I will be charged another 300,000 yuan (USD 43,000) in agent fees on this, and we are required to pay them within a week. After leaving the law firm, I discussed it with my mother. She was very anxious and felt that it would be even less likely to succeed without a good lawyer to represent us! However, there is no way to get such a large amount of money at once. So my mother discussed with the lawyers of Beijing Dayu Law Firm and tried to solve the urgent need of agent fees through an installment payment plan! But unexpectedly...they rejected us.

After being "technically" declined by the lawyers of Dayu to appeal the case, I felt extremely frustrated and helpless. After five years of unjust imprisonment, I was like a worthless garbage, full of grievances and hopelessness. At the same time, my mood was so bad that I even temporarily lost the courage to live. Society has been so unfair to me, and no one understands the injustice and difficulties I suffered. Why is there always no way to ask for help? After adjusting my mentality several times, I embarked on the long road of fighting alone to defend my rights without hesitation.

The first step I have to take is to find its complete evidence and the evidence found must be accurate and true! The official evidence "confirming my guilt" must be mutually corroborated and effectively correspond to each other. Among them, one of the key grounds for my conviction was the accusation that I fabricated that my ex-wife Gao Hong suffered from mental illness. In fact, I did not fabricate her illness. There are not only medical diagnosis paper from Beijing AnDing Hospital and her medication records, but also relevant doctor's appraisal reports, and certificate of sick leave from her employer Air China. As for the reason for my claim, the plaintiff Yashily Int'l kept visiting me in Beijing, asking and tempting me to write it down. They kept asking me to write down additional reasons, saying that only by writing down these reasons would their board of directors take it more seriously and provide more compensation (to my harmed family). Although I defended myself many times, Chaozhou Public Security Bureau, Procuratorate Dept. and Court all ignored it. At that time, I believed that the reason for concocting this unjust case involved political and business collusion behind it. The Chinese dairy "evil forces" must be very powerful! Only in this way can such indiscriminate, total abuse of legal and judicial resources occur.

In Chinese prison, I was placed in solitary confinement and severely abused, leaving me with physical and mental scars. Many of my teeth were knocked out and dropped. My lumbar spine suffered traumatic fractures, and I also suffered from legs spasms, moderate gastric ulcer problems, type 2 diabetes caused by hunger and damage to the peripheral nervous system. At the beginning, I was very blindly obedient to the new environment, but I did not allow myself to be depressed, and I kept encouraging myself and to cheer myself up again.

Starting from seeking for valid evidence, I initiated the verification and tracking process. In August 2014, the second month after I was released from Jieyang prison for a brief recuperation, I sent my first letter of accusation to Guangdong

Guo, Li in front of the Guangzhou Railway Station

Province. After that, I began to travel back and forth to several cities and counties in Guangdong Province where my case was being heard. Until my final appeal for a retrial was successful in August 2016, that is, the 2nd retrial was held in the Guangdong Provincial High Court in Guangzhou, I made a total of more than 30 trips to and from Beijing and Guangdong cities. .

48

From the materials which piles up to nearly a meter high, copied and retrieved from Beijing Dayu Law Firm, Guangdong case-handling Police, Prosecutor and Court offices, I repeatedly read and analyzed the case and compared the evidence collected by myself, through careful study of the case files and my own investigation. After nearly two years, I gained a clear picture and thorough understanding of the entire process of the case. Then I began self-study, studying relevant legal provisions, and learning to write appeal materials and defense statements. During this period, in order to collect facts and evidence about Yashily and Scient Company's counterfeiting of US brand, I went to the United States twice to inquire and collect evidence at the California and Texas registration agencies of Yashily's Scient Inc. in the United States and their accounting firm that had participated in the business registration, found and confirmed the Scient Int'l USA Inc. was deregistered shortly after I was released from prison in 2014.

Because Yashily International was acquired by China Mengniu Dairy Group under COFCO, and both Yashily and Mengniu were listed in the Hong Kong stock market, therefore I came to Hong Kong to collect evidence and continue fight for compensation. At China Mengniu regional office on the 32nd floor of the COFCO Building in Hong Kong, the reception staff said that Yashily, as a Mengniu subsidiary, did not have any employees working there. It only reserves one empty office space at Mengniu Hong Kong and repeatedly noted that Yashily Int'l did not have a physical office on the 32nd floor. Their statement seems false and cannot convince or fool me. Mengniu and Yashily Dairy have not responded after receiving my open letter and claim documents. But I didn't give up, so I went again. When they saw that I was the man who was interviewed and broadcast on Hong Kong TV, they were so afraid that they didn't even dare to let me going through the main gate of their COFCO office building.

All the signs in my evidence collection show guilty Yashily, Mengniu Dairy and their colluded judicial departments are when faced with my wrongful "extortion" case, and how they want to cover it up.

While reading file for the case, I found evidence of fabrication everywhere in the processing. During my appeal process, such evidence was admitted by different level of the courts. In addition to my child harm caused by the melamine baby formula, the judicial abuse environment in which I was exposed actually caused even a deeper harm to me.

In 2016, I traveled frequently between Beijing and Guangdong, just by myself at first. Due to the harsh experience of being held in solitary confinement and being beaten, hungered and abused by the prison guards and their inmate chiefs, I was physically disabled. For this reason, Beijing Civil Affairs Bureau issued me a disability certificate and I received a monthly disability subsidy of 320 yuan (USD46.00). Due to my disability and the lack of a lawyer's aid, I found that many tasks were impossible to be completed on my own, and I had to ask my mother XinHong to act as a case agent. She was already in her 70s at the time, and she traveled tirelessly with me to Chaozhou, Chao'an, Jieyang, Guangzhou, Shenzhen, Hong Kong and other places, leaving the fighting footprints of our life and death together. By the way, I have filed numerous complaints and claims against Guangdong Provincial Procuratorate and Chaozhou Procuratorate for the injuries and tortures I suffered from being beaten, hungered and tortured in prison. In this regard, the relevant responsible parts still shirk the blame in every possible way and refuse to take responsibility for the state compensation, and the relevant "State Compensation" cases of Guo, Li have also made no progress so far.

The process of finding evidence is very difficult. Because of Yashily's strong political and business connections and the highest level of judicial protecting umbrella, no one dared to help me in China. I can only rely on myself to persist, do it bit by bit, and have it completed. According to the timeline provided in the case file, I first found the key or suspicious points, and sorted out and verified the relevant supporting recordings and written materials. Many doubtful points were discovered, including the recordings and witness statements provided by Yashily and Scient negotiators to the police dept, which confirmed that the case was completely confusing right and wrong; the duty police and Yashily colluded with each other to threaten my family in Beijing, before asking them to sign the pre-arranged statements. And if they don't comply, they will also be arrested and sent to jail together with me.

After jigsawing, synthesizing and sorting out all the materials, I did not let go of any clues and tried to figure out the entire context of the case, that is: Yashily proactively contacted the only consumer who was still persisting in fighting to defend his legitimate rights and asked victim's family to submit "a huge amount of money in compensation", and then pretended to negotiate with the family while reporting the case to the police induce me to write a "fictitious and illegal" compensation request package. In this way, a so-called "extortion" case coming from Yashily was concocted.

The recording evidence produced by the Yashily in the case file cannot actually be used to convict me legally. On the contrary, these recording evidence presented their 'lure & trap' process and relevant conclusive evidence about how they

Videos about Guo, Li and his mother meeting with Yashily team

for compensation (actually trap for framing)

committed the crime on us, the victims. The recording clearly recorded the way of how they seduced me and my mother. For example, the recording of our negotiation at CuiGong (or Jade Palace in English) Hotel in Beijing clearly recorded their entire seduction process.

The Yashily and Scient negotiators emphasized to us time and time again: "We want to solve this problem during this visit to your family in Beijing, and we have to have a specific number from you." We said: "Okay, tell us what the situation or stand of yours on this." The Yashily negotiator said: "You can be specific, it'll be fine to us." Then they kept emphasizing to us: "Isn't it just three million yuan, is it…, is it three million yuan of the total package?" They also tried to entice me and my mother to sign in an audio record saying: "How about you writing it down to make it even more clearly? Let's find some papers and a pen to let you write it down." At the Hotel lobby in Beijing where the negotiations were intensely taking place, a CCTV news camera crew indirectly filmed this bargaining process in the bushes from outside the lobby window. They told us: "We are also reporting to our Chairman (Zhang Litian), and Zhang ordered that the writing on paper should be clearer and best to handle this issue with you." "Please JUST sign your name (on the claim paper), and we will go back and talk to him with the papers."

Boss Zhang (Zhang Litian, full name), who they mentioned to us was the president of Guangdong Yashily Int'l

Group, and the chairman of Scient JV (Guangzhou) Company in Guangdong. Also later the chairman of Yashily International, a Chinese dairy giant company listed in Hong Kong. He was a congressman to the National People's Congress at the time. However we still refused to sign on this paper and told them: "You said that Chen Minhui is the director of Yashily's foreign affairs and is from ChaoShan area as well. You two who talked with us can just prove it." But Duan Genghui and Chen said: "You have to sign it absolutely, and we can go back and talk to our boss based on it." We insisted not to sign, said: "Look, Mr. Chen is here as witness on this. Let's make a record and refer to it clearly to your Boss."

The recording also recorded Yashily's subsequent phone calls and come to me voluntarily for negotiations many times. Their motivation is enough to prove: The purpose of Yashily and Scient's offer to negotiate with us further is to find out whether we will continue to use media exposure to disclose them, and to get prepared for their planned false accusations and frame-ups on my legitimate action for the family.

So, before they negotiated the compensation package with us, Yashily & Scient actually reported the case to their hometown police. Because there was no or insufficient evidence to arrest and charge me, they could not file a case properly, therefore they reported the case before collecting the evidence, and kept making corrections at a later stage until they were tempted to tell me the "fictitious and blackmail" content and words they wanted me to say to them, and reached the Chaozhou police they colluded both politically and financially with. After the police dept. helped them preset the conditions for filing a criminal case like this, in the name of rule of laws in China: I was caught like a turtle dropped in a jar. Their aim to cover up the truth and achieving the goal of concealing the truth succeeded.

One of the recordings before their arrest of me in Hangzhou, Zhejiang province shows Yashily's negotiator Duan and their senior managers shouting: "We must have him caught and killed this time! I hope you will return in triumph, and I will boost your courage on this." "We are here to put him in our trap and let him die in jail."

These false accusations and frame-up plans and actions applied were all evidenced by the recordings provided by Yashily themselves. Obviously, these evidences collected are evidence of Yashily's own crimes. Not only can they not prove an alleged extortion, but they can prove that they are making false accusations and frame-ups on me. What's ridiculous or funny is that Chaozhou's judiciaries cooperated with Yashily openly, deliberately obfuscated and accepted them as false evidence. The only explanation is that Yashily (nicknamed as "An Evil Forces") has long been colluded with the local government and justice depts. for an evil purpose! This unjust case was concocted because they were determined to win. In the end, no one expected that I would persist, expose and appeal after being released from arduous five years

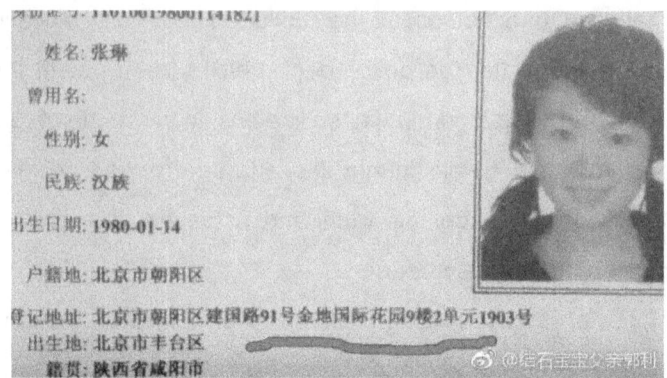

The personal information even address provided by Zhang, Lin to police is verified be false and fake.

imprisonment.

I read the materials in the case file one by one. And a former lawyer told me from her professional perspective that there was a lady called Zhang Lin who was adding fuel to the flames on this case. Ms. Zhang is my ex-wife's colleague and friend. I only met her once, when she wanted to borrow some foreign currency from me one time, but I declined. Later, when she heard that our kid fell ill due to taking Yashily's tainted-baby formula, she offered to help us.

According to the reporting materials provided by Yashily and the case handling records of the Chao'an Police in Guangdong, ZhangLin is my wife's former colleague of Air China in Beijing and a friend. She provided witness statements for Yashily, including her current work and home addresses. I went to find her based on these filed info and found that the information she used for filing of the case were all false and faked, this shows the question on authenticity and reliability of the testimony she provided. Later from the records, I found out that Zhang had a business relationship with Yashily on advertising, and she wanted to represent Yashily for its dairy advertising businesses in the mainland China. The impact and aftermath of China "melamine milk" scandal was so tremendous that it also affected Zhang Lin's company business on dairy advertising. As a result, Zhang and Yashily took this opportunity to collude and play a double-'reed'-performance each other. The document states that She, ZhangLin, even advised Yashily management to report the "crime" to the police on blackmail. And this couldn't just be a Zhang's own idea. In the recording, Zhang said: "He, Guo, Li just wants to use this incident to blackmail you and then ask for more compensation, and if you give him the money, he will not stop. After signing the agreement, he should have stopped, but he didn't, and they are still doing it." "Everything Guo, Li has done is to make Yashily Group lose more money, so Yashily should immediately take corresponding legal means to charge against him. Why doesn't your company sue him for extortion?"

During the verification process, I also discovered a sad thing, that is, one week before my arrest, my ex-wife wrote a statement to the board of directors of Yashily behind my back, claiming that she was firmly opposed to my legal actions. What shocked me even more was that she also wrote in the statement that our child was in good health conditions and showed no any symptoms related to melamine formula issue.

This is weird. When she or even together with her mother TaoXin took our baby child to the hospital for Type B ultrasonic, health examination and medical treatment, I followed them. She also took our child to the hospital several times alone, and all these had medical records and diagnoses reports. How did it suddenly turn out that the harmed child had no symptoms? Could it be that with just one statement from her, the judicial authorities of Guangdong could put Beijing Children's Research Institute and Beijing Children's Hospital, which had performed the examination on the child, and even Haidian Maternity & Children's Hospital, which was responsible for having the screening, type B-ultrasounds, urine test, and blood lab reports that have been issued to be overturned? The statement made by my ex-wife is obviously a false one made to fully cooperate with the judiciary of Guangdong in concocting an unjust case. However, even the worst thing is that the two levels of courts in Chaozhou actually violated the rule of law principle during the trial sessions and the false evidence was admitted to against me! It was this false statement that played a certain "catalyst" role in my conviction and imprisonment.

For this matter, after I was released from Jieyang prison, TaoXin, my child's grandmother specifically said to me: "Li, there are some things I want to explain to you." I said: "What do you need to explain?" She said: "Actually when they were asked to sign or record on the police papers, many of them were not read clearly or carefully. Cause they didn't give them time to read and check". In fact, the Guangdong police came to Beijing and forced her to sign the papers, so she just signed them. "I can understand you." I forgave her for this reason. Even if my family members say I did commit a crime, I can understand and forgive them. But I absolutely cannot forgive them for deceiving themselves and saying that my child was not harmed. This is always my consistent principle and it's the bottom line.

After I was released from prison, I approached my ex-wife about custody of our child and aftermath of her health plus state compensation issues, but both she and her family were reluctant and rejected me. I also respect her because after all she has started a new family. I went to see her several times, but she didn't want to meet or talk about more on the future of our child, so I gave up.

Regarding my ex-wife's false testimony, I look at it from two aspects. On the one hand, of course from an emotional point of view, I don't want to directly hold her responsible, I just hope she can understand the truth. I also asked her family to tell her that I hope she can surrender herself and explain clearly the circumstances under which she wrote that "false" statement and why she wrote it to Yashily. The wrongful conviction caused to "somewhat" extent by her witness testimony is another (criminal case) issue. The reason I suggested she turn herself in was that I was afraid she would become a scapegoat of Mengniu Yashily in future. Because I can see the case files and see something deeper inside this case. But my ex-wife can't see them. So I hope she can take the initiative to stand up and tell the truth as soon as possible, so that she can protect herself and not be used as cannon fodder for Mengniu Yashily, the evil forces in Chinese dairy industry. On the other hand, I also forgive her. I can understand a woman who chooses to protect herself when she is threatened by taking sides in politics. Therefore, when I was interviewed by the media, I never said that I would pursue her, and I did not include her name in the list of major suspects who were accused of falsely charging me.

In addition, I also clarified a legal basis: the three million yuan compensation we proposed against to Yashily at that time was legal and protected by the law as long as consumers were harmed or injured by the infringer, and it does not belong to the extortion of criminal code at all. It cannot be even attributed to a criminal case.

When I was making appeals and accusations against injustices after I was released from prison, some lawyers wanted to help me, and I also found a few well-known lawyers. However, during the specific communication process, after these lawyers discovered Yashily's political and business power and its CCP state-level leader background, they backed down out of fear, some of them even tried to persuade me to give up. There were also some lawyers who wanted to make money and attract public attention, demanding high agency fees from me. There are also some lawyers who I think their professional knowledge and character are too poor to pass the test. There was also a law firm that expressed its willingness to take one of my cases, but the condition was that it must publicly declare that my mother XinHong was their contract staff. Then I laughed: Okay, then you will pay my mother half a year's salary first, so that you can start our legal service business in accordance with the law. After much thinking, I did not choose any lawyer. My case was fought on my own, through my mother and myself. I checked the evidence materials by myself and asked my friends such as Tina YZ to help sort them out. Although it is very difficult, there is always a strong force in my heart that supports me keep going forward.

I went to Chao'an County Court and Chaozhou Intermediate Court of Guangdong Province to review the files, but I encountered various difficulties from them. However I always insisted on checking and copying all the files according to the law, until they had no choice but agreed. In the end, I was able to access and copy almost all the files they have for this case. Faced with a pile of case file materials, I feel difficult to get started. Some materials alone have more than 20,000 words. Imagine that the prosecutor and judge in charge of the case would not have read these materials completely if they had no patience. During my second instance appeal, the court ruling was just issued within a few days. The judge may not have "good" enough time to review the case. But these are nothing compared to the physical and mental torture and abuse I suffered in their detention centers and prisons when I totally lost my freedom. These hardships cannot defeat me!

Fortunately, my mother understands me very well. Though she is getting old and in a poor health condition, but she still stands with me and has always supported me firmly.

In order to collect information on my "State Compensation Case" for Jieyang prison, I returned to Jieyang of Guangdong where I had been wrongfully imprisoned for nearly four years. My mood at that time was really mixed. But I went back again, not as a "criminal" but as a free citizen and human rights defender. For the sake of justice in my heart and to win back my innocence, I went to collect evidence from the Jieyang prison management. When a prison guard who had disciplined me before saw me there, he stood up to attention with a snap, which surprised me. I couldn't help but look up him. His police hat was squared, no longer like hanging diagonally on the top of his head before. His uniform is also neatly worn and snugly fitted. The buttons on his shirt underneath are tightly buttoned, his leather shoes also look clean and shiny, and the belt around his waist is tied neatly and his face appeared very tense and serious. It's not like the hooligans with sideways eyes, grinning mouth, and cigarette in hand that I've seen them inside the prison before. I couldn't help but raise my right hand to straighten his police uniform. Meanwhile I praised him: "You look very good today." He smiled sheepishly, put down his saluting hand, turned around and bent down to support me and my mother.

I saw a few more prison guards along the way to the prison head office. As soon as they saw me, they immediately stood at attention against the wall and straightened their backs. When I arrived at the prison head office, we knocked on the door and the door opened. When the person inside saw it was me, he immediately straightened his clothes and his sitting posture, and put his hands on his legs. His previous "bossy manner" appearance was totally gone. Although the scene at that time was constantly intertwined with the scene when I was in prison, my mind was extremely peaceful. Judging from their expressions and actions, they now truly regard me as a human being (not an animal), and feel a little remorse or fearful in their hearts; at the same time, I am afraid they have to admire me as a true fighter with capital letters from the bottom of their hearts. And their changing seems to be a transformation of human nature.

After I was released from Jieyang prison, I have been on the road to continue defending my rights. I often wear a white T-shirt or hoody with a poster about me on the cover of major world media. After spending years in the darkest prison cells, my eyes are afraid of sunlight, so I wear sunglasses during daily outdoor activities. Because my spine on the lower back was hit hard to be fractured by the cell-chiefs in jail, my legs and feet are often cramping and spasms during the nights, my body cannot bear weight, and I walk unsteady and need to use a walking cane. And such dress-up looks very strange to outsiders. Passers-by often look at me curiously. But I spoke to myself: Oh, it doesn't matter. I've been in jail already, so what do I care? In this way, I visited the relevant political part and judiciary departments, even the National People's Congress Standing Committee and other CCP departments in Guangzhou, Chaozhou and Shenzhen, submitted reports, accusations and complaints to the courts and the tribunal of the PRC Supreme Court in Guangdong province.

On May 21st 2015, Guangdong Provincial High Court issued my case retrial decision for the second time, ruling that the facts of the original trials and 1st retrial were unclear and the evidence of conviction was insufficient. This time, the retrial

Guo, Li asking for State Compensations
from Jieyang Prison in Guangdong

court was switched to the Provincial High Court itself. It is extremely rare in Chinese modern history for a retrial case to be heard by the Provincial High Court itself, which I encountered unexpectedly. The Provincial High Court held that: Scient JV and Yashily Group took the initiative to contact Guo, Li, the victim and Guo made a package (claim) request for the category and amount of compensation, which fell within the scope of civil dispute matter.

## Chapter 5.

# Collecting evidences, restoring the truth, and changed the verdict to not a guilty

On August 8th 2016, just more than two years after I was released from prison, Guangdong Provincial High Court held a hearing on this case. Guangdong Provincial Procuratorate issued a prosecutorial opinion which consisted of two pages. I still remember every word of it by heart. The title is: Opinions of the Prosecutor's Appearance in the Retrial Case of Guangdong Provincial People's Procuratorate.

【Text】 Presiding Judge, Judge: According to Article 245 of the Criminal Procedure Law of the People's Republic of China, we are appointed by Guangdong Provincial People's Procuratorate to represent this case in the court. We perform our duties in accordance with the law in Guangdong Provincial High Court's retrial of the original appellant Guo, Li's extortion case. In order to enable the court to review the facts of this case, accurately apply the Chinese law, and make a fair judgment on the appellant in the original trial, the following court opinions are hereby issued on the facts and evidence of the case.

Your attention to the Court:

1. The existing evidence is insufficient to prove that the appellant Guo, Li in the original trial had the subjective purpose of illegal possession. According to Article 274 of the Criminal Procedure Law of the People's Republic of China, the crime of extortion is to threaten or intimidate others for the purpose of illegal possession, to seize a large amount of public or private property, or to commit multiple acts of extortion. The purpose

of illegal possession refers to illegal possession, or intention to possess the other part's property based on legal basis. In this case, first of all, the child of the original appellant Guo, Li, consumed Scient baby formula containing melamine. After a health examination by BTPZ Hospital in Haidian District of Beijing, it was confirmed that multiple punctate strong echoes were visible in the central collecting system of the child kidneys. , proving that her body was harmed by Yashily's Scient dairy product. As Guo, Li is his child's guardian, he has the legal right to claim compensation from the dairy manufacturer. His claim has a legal basis and has a legitimate purpose.

Secondly, Guo received RMB 400,000 (~USD 57,000) of compensation in payment from Scient JV Company, and Guo, Li promised not to pursue the lawsuit and gave up his claim for compensation. Afterwards, Guo, Li once again raised a claim of RMB 3 million (~USD 428,000) to see if he had lost the legitimacy of the purpose. The original 1st retrial effective judgment held that this 'updated' amount is difficult to determine as a legitimate request to compensate for injury and harm, and Guo, Li has the subjective purpose of illegal possession. Regarding this point, we, the procurators believes that the original judgment confused the difference between rights and the objects to which rights refer, and wrongly used the amount of the objects as the criterion for determining the existence of rights. There is a legal relationship of infringement between the baby formula manufacturer and Guo's child. Guo has the right to claim compensation according to law. The family representative Guo, Li will make claims based on the infringement facts on behalf of his harmed child, regardless of the target. Regardless of the amount of the claim, the number of times for the claim, it is an exercise of Guo's right to claim and does not affect the legitimacy of his purpose. As for whether Guo violated the principle of good faith, whether his claim for three million yuan (~USD 428,000) can be realized will be determined by negotiation between the two parts concerned, or the law court will make a judgment in accordance with the Chinese law. Before that, it was a controversial civil legal issue. And Guo claimed three million yuan in compensation, is a way to exercise his civil rights and does not belong to the purpose of illegal possession.

2. The behavior of the appellant Guo, Li in the original trial did not meet the objective requirements of the criminal law of extortion. During the claim process, Guo proposed to Yashily Int'l Group and Scient JV Company that if their family demands were not met, negative reports would be made through domestic and foreign media, which would expand the impact and make the two companies uncontrollable or even go bankrupt. This shows Guo's behavior, the method of defending is to threaten exposure to the media. According to Article 6 of the <Chinese Consumer Rights & Interests Protection Law>, the Law encourages and supports all organizations and individuals to conduct social supervision of business behaviors

that harm the legitimate rights and interests of consumers. The mass media should do a good job in publicity to safeguard the legitimate rights and interests of consumers, and conduct publicity on actions that harm the legitimate rights and interests of consumers. Acts of legitimate rights and interests shall be subject to public opinion supervision. Therefore, consumers have the right to expose and criticize the business behaviors

广东省人民检察院
**再审案件出庭检察员意见书**

64

审判长、审判员：

根据《中华人民共和国刑事诉讼法》第二百四十五条的规定，我们受广东省人民检察院指派，代表本院，出席本法庭，对广东省高级人民法院提审原审上诉人郭利敲诈勒索一案依法执行职务，为使法庭查清案件事实，准确适用法律，对原审上诉人作出公正的判决，现就案件的事实、证据，发表如下出庭意见，请法庭注意。

一、现有证据不足以证实原审上诉人郭利主观上具有非法占有的目的。根据《中华人民共和国刑法》第二百七十四条的规定，敲诈勒索罪，是以非法占有为目的，对他人实施威胁、恐吓，索取公私财物数额较大或者多次敲诈勒索的行为。非法占有的目的，是指无法律依据而意图占有对方财产。本案中，首先，原审上诉人郭利的女儿郭某某食用了含三聚氰胺的"施恩"牌奶粉，经北京市海淀区北太平庄医院检查，证实郭某某"双肾中央集合系统内可见数个点状强回声"，证明郭某某的身体受到"施恩"牌奶粉的侵害，郭利作为郭某某的法定监护人，有权利向奶粉的生产厂家索赔，其索赔行为有法律依据，具有目的的正当性。其次，

The first page of Opinions of the Prosecutor's Appearance in the Retrial Case of Guangdong Provincial People's Procuratorate.

that harm their rights and interests through mass media.

Guo, Li's threat to be shown to the media was reasonable and legal, and did not meet the objective behavioral requirements for extortion. To sum up, the behavior of the appellant Guo, Li in the original trial did not meet the subjective and objective elements of the crime of extortion, and his behavior did not constitute the crime of extortion. The Chaozhou Intermediate People's Court (2010) ChaoZhongFa XingZaiZi No. 1 Criminal Ruling made an error in sentencing and convicting Guo, Li. In order to ensure the unity and correct implementation of the law, maintain judicial fairness, accurately punish crimes, and protect the legitimate rights of the defendant, the above prosecutorial opinions are put forward in accordance with Article 245, Section 2 of the Criminal Procedure Law of the People's Republic of China. The collegial panel should give full consideration and make a fair judgment on Guo in accordance with the law.

Delivered a speech in the High court.    Signed by: Guangdong Provincial People's Procuratorate.

As a witness in this case, my mother XinHong stated what really happened to the court and the prosecutor. It proves that the entire claim process was conducted in an invited, open and transparent manner and with the knowledge of the victim's family, Yashily & Scient and the reporting media, and that we, as the victims did not commit any extortion.

Due to the high level of social concern over "melamine

milk" scandal in China, my appeal for 2nd retrial was filed and accepted until the court session, which attracted the attention of many media. Regarding my case, the well-known Chinese media named Caixin has made several exclusive reports on it.

During the interview, a senior reporter analyzed the case with me. Considering the judicial environment at the time and the political business background of Yashily and Scient Joint Venture's favor in Guangdong, he felt that the possibility of changing my acquittal was very slim, but I was not discouraged. Difficulties are not a reason to stop me from moving forward. On the contrary, they are my motivation; the more difficulties there are, the more they prove the meaning of my persistence.

After the retrial and the verdict was changed to not guilty, a lawyer from so called "XU Zhiyong* Lawyers' Team" came to me. This lawyers' team represented a family group of about 50 babies and young children who were victims of the "melamine

## Caixin

Dec 04, 2019 02:58 PM
POLITICS & LAW

## Father Seeks Compensation From Mengniu for Milk Tainting Scandal

By Michael Smith

Screenshot of Caixin report on Guo, Li's case

Famous lawyer Xu Zhiyong

baby formula" scandals involving Yashily & Scient products. After the melamine incident came to light in 2008, these babies and young children who were suspected of being poisoned by consuming Yashily and Scient milk powder and their parents jointly entrusted XU Zhiyong's team to act as their counsel to defend their legal rights and claim through a class sue in Beijing. At that time, the biggest obstacle and problem they encountered in safeguarding their rights was the lack of solid evidence like mine who could personally obtain evidence from the authoritative food safety inspection department of the General Administration of Quality Supervision, Inspection and Quarantine on whether the consumed formula had quality and safety problems. At that time, assistants from XU Zhiyong's team like LIN Zheng, lawyer PENG Jian, and lawyer HOU came to me and asked for help. At that time, I did not hesitate at all and gave a photocopy of Yashily's Scient baby formula test & appraisal report I obtained from inspections at my own

Guo, Li standing in front of Yashily's gate

in Chaozhou, Guangdong

costs to other harmed babies and young children.

After I was released from prison, one day a lawyer called Peng Jian from XU Zhiyong's team met with me in a cafe in Beijing and told me about the progress and results of their a class-sued Yashily & Scient tainted-baby formula case that they had represented after my arrest in 2009. At that time, Yashily & Scient sent its corporate counsels like Wu Xiaonan to them after finding out the alumni connection of China University of Political Science and Law (中国政法大学) in Beijing. They took an emergency flight from Guangzhou to Beijing with more than three million yuan in cash and made a special appointment with XU's team to discuss the legal issues with dozens of victim families, together with compensation issues and the parts concerned worked together to reach a "Settlement Agreement". According to his introduction, the agreement stipulates that Yashily & Scient are willing to make one-time compensation to the families of harmed infants and young children who plan to participate in this class-sue action. The class-plaintiff and their lawyers have challenged Yashily & Scient regarding the suspected consumption of Yashily and Scient products containing melamine. For the harm caused by the formula to the infants and young children of the plaintiff's family, the lawsuit was agreed to be withdrawn from Beijing Haidian District Court right after the settlement issue was resolved, also the class-plaintiff and their lawyers were not allowed to sue or claim against the manufacturers for compensation again. The lawyers could no longer represent the plaintiffs of harmed children for such kind of formula cases in China.

In this regard, more than 50 family parents and their

lawyers signed the "Settlement Agreement" with Yashily & Scient. However, when we met at the café, PengJian, one of the lawyers in the legal team, kept expressing their remorse to me, saying that they had violated the original intention (conscience) of the lawyer's practice by signing the "Settlement Agreement" with Yashily & Scient. In fact, they had betrayed the legitimate rights and interests of the children and the future of China's food safety in exchange for a "Settlement Agreement" issued by the baby formula manufacturers, and made undue compromises and did not insist on fighting against their will, so they felt regretful and uneasy. In the end, he further affirmed that "Guo, it is right for you to insist on fighting unyieldingly, and you are not back down in front of the 'evil forces'." "China lacks a warrior like you, and China's food safety and judicial environment must be as persistent as you to have real hope and safety. If people all do like what we did for the 50 victim families, China's food safety problem will end up in a situation where there is still no safety guarantee at all! Yashily (evil forces) will continue to make the formula even worse......

Although XU Zhiyong's lawyer team has not been of any help to me in my wrongfully imprisoned case, it is undoubtedly a compliment and encouragement for me to be recognized by his professional team after I was released from prison.

There was an episode, that is, for a considerable period of time after the Guangdong Provincial High Court and the Provincial Procuratorate filed and accepted the case, opened a court to retry the case, and issued a prosecutorial opinion, there was no progress in the case anymore.

During this period, I went to Europe. I had originally booked a round-trip economy class ticket operated by China Hainan Airlines. I was transferring from France to Brussels Airport in Belgium in returning route. When I wanted to check in at the airport, I was stopped by the Brussels Airport staff. I was told that there was no ticket booked for a person called Guo, Li in their civil aviation computer customer system. After repeated inquiries, a person in charge of the airport contacted a representative of Hainan Airlines for me. After checking my information, the representative said: Mr. Guo, there is really no your ticket booking information for the current flight. But it doesn't matter, if you have to go back China right now, the company can temporarily arrange a first-class seat for you. I was anxious when I heard this, because I bought the last row of economy class at very low price. If I wanted to upgrade to first class by myself, I would have to pay the price difference of nearly 20,000 yuan （~USD 2,850.00）. So I said in confusion: I bought an economy class ticket, why do you want to upgrade me at will? As a result, the representative added: Mr. Guo, the upgrade we give you is free and you don't need to pay any additional fees.

Shortly after returning to China, I learned that the airline company had received instructions from relevant higher ranking department within its internal control system that I was considered "guilty" and that I would not return Beijing after this visiting abroad. For this reason, they cancelled my returning ticket in advance.

Shortly after I was released from prison in August 2014, I took a train to Guangzhou for business. On the way, I wanted to discuss the issue of the compensation owed by Yashily's Sino-US Scient JV Company. After many years, Yashily Group has undergone frequent personnel changes, and it looks like it has changed beyond recognition. When I first arrived at their office building, the security guards and staff of Chuangju Business Tower forcibly blocked me from going up to the 12th floor of its office. During this period, perhaps due to domestic and foreign medias following me, when I went to Yashily office again, the security guard of the building just let me go directly and seemed to turn a blind eye to me! Hundreds of office workers in the entire group were panicked when they saw me,

Guo, Li showing papers marked as Poison-baby formula Yashily etc.

in front of Yashily/ Scient office tower in Guangzhou

hiding around and not daring to face me. The entire floor office area of Scient Co. in Guangzhou instantly turned into a desert, and all the staff at their workstations ran away in advance. I submitted an open letter to the front desk and asking the person in charge of their legal dept to forward it to Yashily and Scient's board of directors. However, none of them, including its lawyers, dared to take the letter.

Finally, I found the legal department again, but it seems that Wu Xiaonan, the former corporate lawyer, no longer works at Yashily or Scient. The staff in the legal department now say that they don't know about my case at all. At first I thought they were evading on purpose, but later I found out that they were indeed "uninformed." Just before and after the second retrial proceedings, the legal department of Scient Company did send a letter to Guangdong Provincial High Court, requesting "to know the detailed facts and full disclosure of my case."

On August 8th 2016, Guangdong Provincial High Court held a retrial on Guo, Li's "extortion" case. In court, the prosecutor held the point that no matter how much the claim was, it was Guo, Li who was exercising his lawful rights to claim. If the formula manufacturer did not agree with the amount of his claim, it would be a controversial civil legal dispute. Guo, Li's claim behavior and the amount of the claim did not affect the legitimacy of his purpose. Guo, Li's behavior did not constitute the crime of extortion, and the original judgment on Guo, Li's conviction and sentencing was totally wrong. After several hours of trial, the court announced that it would set a date for sentencing.

At this point, the change of acquittal ushered in the dawn. Since then, many media have launched "indiscriminate bombardment" reports on this 2nd retrial. On August 25th 2016,

Other media's reports on Guo, Li's case

a most popular weekly newspaper in south China "NanFangZhouMo" (南方周末报, Southern Weekend Newspaper), published a special article reporting 【The Last "Melamine" Rights Defender in China"】

On August 26th, the infzm.com (南方周末 in Chinese, Southern Weekend Newspaper) published another article and conducted interviews with some well-known legal figures. According to Zhang Yansheng, my original first-instance defense lawyer, Scient & Yashily dairy designed a "fishing negotiation trap" to induce Guo Li to take the bait. She believes that the Chinese law stipulates that for consumers to become

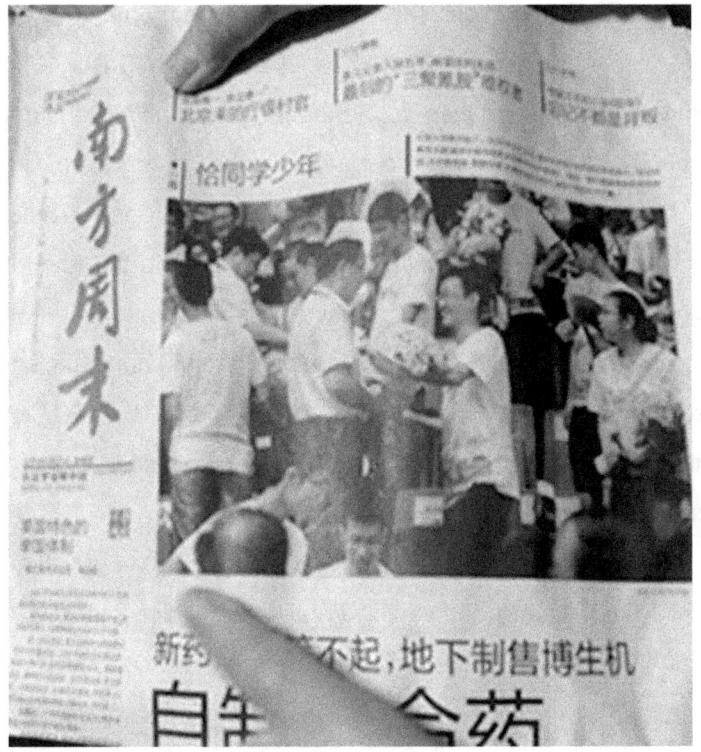

Photo of 南方周末, Southern Weekend Newspaper

which has the report of Guo, Li's case

the criminal subject of extortion crimes, they must meet two conditions at the same time: the content of the transaction proposed to the merchant is illegal, and the means of transaction with the merchant are illegal. In the Guo's case, He claimed compensation from the illegal manufacturers through negotiation or litigation, and exposed the illegal activities of the illegal manufacturers to the news media. This is the legal right granted to him as consumers by the law. Guo neither used threats nor obtained illegal "shut-up fee" or illegal property, so the crime of "extortion" cannot be established. Zhang's views are also recognized by many legal experts in China. Chen Beiyuan, a legal counsel to Guangdong Provincial Consumer Council, also believes: "As a family member of the victim, Guo, Li has the right to file financial compensation against Scient Company. Before the court makes a judgment, the law fully allows consumers and businesses to negotiate for compensation, even if there is nothing wrong with claiming a 100 million Yuan (~USD 14,280,000). This is a typical civil dispute issue, and it is obviously wrong to escalate it to a criminal case."

With public doubts that Yashily's "fishing negotiations" lured Guo, Li into committing crimes, Lin Jinlin, manager of Yashily's Public Relations & Media Center, responded to the medias, saying that all evidence collection and litigation conducted by Yashily Group were legal. After the second instance of Chaozhou Intermediate Court in 2010, Guo, Li's case received a rare opportunity for a (1st) retrial, but the verdict was not overturned. Therefore, there is no problem with the court's verdict. He said he believed that the Guangdong Provincial High Court would also make a fair judgment, and justice would prevail in people's hearts. Lin said: After China tainted-baby-formula incident broke out, Guo, Li took his two-year-old child to BTPZ Hospital in Haidian District, Beijing for a Type B-ultrasound screening which showed that "multiple punctate strong echoes can be seen in the central collecting system of both kidneys." The kidney function of the child patient has been severely damaged. However, this hospital is not one of five secondary hospitals designated by Beijing Health Bureau for (final) diagnosis. But at that time, our company gave in to Guo and first paid a compensation of RMB 400,000 (~USD 57,000) to his family. Lin also added that throughout the entire issue, Yashily had always maintained communication with Guo, but his family's unreasonable demands had "beyond the bottom-line of what our company can tolerate." He emphasized: "Of course, we, Yashily, hope to handle the dispute issue through civil means, but Guo has brought our companies to the forefront of public opinion AGAIN! Therefore we are forced to have no choice but to use the most extreme and violent means to deal with HIM."

With the issue of jurisdiction of this case, a reporter asked: "Why the case should be tried in Chao'an County of Guangdong, where Yashily Group is located? Since the judgment also mentioned that Yashily and Scient are two independent companies, why is the case not trialed in Guangzhou, where Scient JV Company located?" Some lawyers asked, "Is this suspected of using the local judicial system to retaliate against Guo Li?" Lin Jinlin explained: "The company lacks relevant experience."

Finally, Lin Jinlin told the media: "Had we known there would be such a situation, we would not have made such a (bad) choice."

I have been waiting for these words for eight years.

Eight months later, on April 7th 2017, Guangdong Provincial High Court held a second hearing on the 2nd retrial of my "extortion" case. During the retrial, I submitted relevant facts and innocent evidence to the Court, and also stated my prepared defense papers and concluded remarks. After more than an hour of closed-door discussion, they cleared out reporters who presented in advance, the judge pronounced in court: The facts of Guo, Li's forcible extortion of finances were unclear and the evidence is insufficient. According to the existing evidence, the nature of Guo's behavior does not exceed the scope of civil disputes, and Guo cannot be found guilty of extortion. The rulings and judgments of the former Chaozhou Intermediate Court and Chao'an County Court are revoked. The defendant Guo, Li in the original trial is not guilty and can apply for his state compensation within two years after his acquittal according to the China State Compensation Law.

At 15:00 pm on the same day, in the 9th Court of Guangdong Provincial High Court, I signed on the final sentencing transcript of (2015) Yue Gao Fa Sheng Xing Jian Zai Zi No.19 and wrote "The truth always exists, and the law always exists" (真理常存,法理常在) in eight big Chinese characters.

The moment I received the verdict of being not-guilty, I really felt in sadness and somewhat in real peace. I was not excited, surprised or satisfied with the result at all. It's been too long, for eight years, eight whole years of my golden time have been wasted!

That day, many media teams were waiting outside the court main gate. After 16:00 p.m., I accepted an interview with China Central Television (CCTV), and they produced a special report program entitled "Guo, Li, the wrongly-imprisoned victim

96

广 东 省 高 级 人 民 法 院

宣 判 笔 录

（2015）粤高法审监刑再字第 19 号

时间： 2017 年 4 月 7 日 15 时 00 分

地点： 本院三楼第九法庭

审判人员： 李华、王兴光、池基浩

书记员： 邓艳美

公诉人（检察员）： 蒙艳

到庭的当事人和其他诉讼参与人： 郭利

审判长宣读广东省高级人民法院（2015）粤高法审监刑再字第 19 号刑事判决书，并告知根据《国家赔偿法》的有关规定，在收到判决书后，可以依法申请国家赔偿。

宣判后当事人的表举：

_（handwritten）_

当事人签名（手印） _（signature）_ 2017 4 7 15 40

审判人员签名：

书记员签名：

The Court Record of Declaring Guo`s Innocent and Qualifications of

China State Compensation Issue

of melamine-tainted baby formula: This was a well-planned and framed case." I remember what I said at that time: "My name is Guo, Li, the father of a baby who was harmed by melamine. When I defended my family's rights, I was sued for extortion and was wrongfully imprisoned for five years. At the same time, I was also a victim of a five year prison sentence for the melamine-milk powder case in China."

Therefore, after being released from prison in 2014, I continued to walk on the road of civil rights defending for myself. My case was 'carefully' designed and concocted by members of the board of directors of Yashily Group and its affiliated companies, as well as some key officials from the Police, Procuratorate, and Law-courts in Guangdong. I want to clarify through media on how I was able to file a 2nd retrial case in between 2013-2015 and fight against the unjust case, and finally get the current acquittal. This is what I am mainly talking about today."

The day after my acquittal was made, Ms. Jiang Yalin, a Guizhou mom who actively participated in collective rights defending for the sicken children at that time in Zhejiang province, invited me to meet her in Shanghai. A journals' team from Shanghai TV Kankan News accompanied me there. Ms. Jiang said that her child's kidney-stones have not been completely eliminated yet. It is like a time-bomb, you don't know when it will explode. She also added that she admired my rigorous work style, and she did not have the capability, the same evidence and ideas as I had. At that time, she believed that her child's edible food was baby formula, and the diagnosis of kidney-stones from their child was the best proof of the quality problem with dairy of Dumex (多美滋) baby formula. She did not keep the receipts for purchasing the formula product and was not in a position to identify the melamine level in the dairy product. When she learned that the "Dumex" baby formula her child had eaten and was distributed in Shanghai by a wholly foreign-owned business, was not among the 68 batches of problematic baby-formula announced, although she found more than 200 parents of babies with kidney stones' problem who had eaten similar milk product and tried to find a way to collectively defend their rights, The court refused to accept their case(s), and the petitions yielded no results. In addition, she and other parents once raised funds

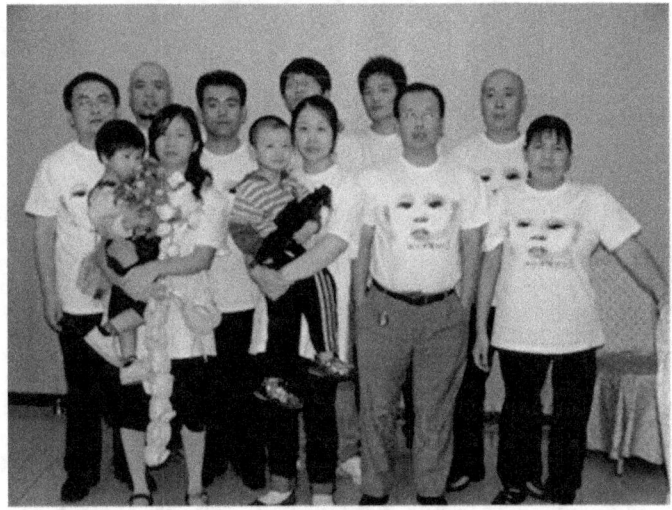

Other suspected poison-baby-formula victim families with lawyers

for a parent in Hangzhou of Zhejiang province to do a baby formula inspection, but the parent subsequently lost contact and the task was abandoned. What's even more ridiculous is that Ms. Jiang's husband, because he was afraid of having trouble on the fight, took the opportunity to hand over some of the remaining evidence related to their child's formula issues (such as T-shirts with demonstration logos) to WeiWenBan (local social stability agency) behind her back.

One victim of poison-formula baby and the mother

At that time, some parents of harmed babies with stone problems who had eaten Scient baby formula received compensation higher than the "China national standard" of 2,000 yuan (~USD300.00). Jiang Yalin also confirmed to reporters the settlement between Yashily & Scient Companies and other parents in Beijing. However, it is difficult for other formula victims to make progress in defending their rights. Based on this, I told news in Shanghai that other parents whose children consumed Scient dairy product would receive that pitiful additional compensation based on the results of unqualified formula quality inspection report containing 132.9mg/kg of "melamine" that I had provided to their lawyers in the class lawsuit at Beijing.

After the news of Guo, Li's successful reversal of the case and his acquittal was announced, GongSun Xue, the lawyer who represented me in the first instance, made a special appointment to meet with me. As explaining the reasons for refusing to represent me in the appeal case at the beginning of 2015, lawyer GongSun also gave a detailed explanation. She said that at the same time that they were preparing to represent me in the case, their law firm also had another three cases in which they pleaded not guilty and took over. However, in the final defense of innocence and state compensation issues (like the NianBin case), all three cases failed. The lawyers who were at a low point unanimously judged that the chance of success in my case of appeal was extremely low and that the chance of win were down to zero, and it was impossible to be successful on it! And... they have NO faith.

When I approached them for help shortly after I was released from Guangdong prison in 2014, although I expressed the idea of continuing to appeal from Beijing, when they saw my unwavering determination and felt that it was impossible to persuade me to give up, they took advantage of this to ask for a high appeal agency fee with rather harsh conditions. In addition, my mother and I had to pay the lawyer fees in one lump sum within a week before they could start working as my lawyer. Lawyer Gongsun later emphasized: "The purpose of Beijing Dayu Law Firm was actually to make you retreat from the difficulties or challenges at that time. Because we have no confidence in the Chinese justice at all! Unexpectedly, now, relying on your own resilience and persistence, you, Guo, Li, has done what our lawyers think is impossible, but you have succeeded." Hearing such a sincere explanation and self-reproach from a lawyer, I suddenly felt extremely disappointed in the heart. Just imaging, even legal workers in China have given up the pursuit of truth, fairness and justice, so the road of defending the rights of ordinary Chinese people can be imagined to be so difficult and arduous, and it is even more difficult than going to the space!

Looking back at 2008, the "melamine-tainted" baby formula incident in China was not only a domestic issue, but also a worldwide one. It has affected tens of millions of victimized families inside and outside the country. The Chinese parents of the "stone-babies" have been organizing fight-through-class sue groups to defend their legal rights for their children for many years, and 16 years have passed now. In the long and torturous process of survival, many rights activists were gradually disintegrated and fallen apart, some escaped from their cages to the free world, and some almost disappeared in sight. In the end, I was left as a lonely warrior, fighting alone, struggling myself, and keeping firm & inflexible.

The unjust case was really overturned, so I was named "the father of the kidney-stone baby", "the lonely fighter for defending (human) rights", "the hero of civil rights defending", "the backbone of Chinese nation" and "the lonely brave man " by the Chinese people and government medias. However, after five years in prison, three years of appeal and protests after being released, plus six years of "State Compensation Case(s)" procedure to pursue the responsibility of Guangdong Provincial Police, Procuratorate, Court and Prison (公检法 in Chinese ) as the tort-authorities obligated to pay my compensation(s), the young and middle-aged prime years who have been wiped out in the past 16 years, and the inhuman treatment and torture to my physical and mind that have been disabled and sicken in purgatory. These pains are indelible and

The family photo of Guo, Li

eternal memories.

It turned out that my little warm family was gone, and I have been a stranger to my child, not as her father. I feel guilty that not only was I missing the five-year father's role in her life, but also that the 'middle and high-level social' connections, the 'glamorous' job, and the 'middle-class decent' life seemed to have nothing to do with me now. I picked up the phone in my hand, looked at the unfamiliar numbers, and wanted to contact my former colleagues and friends to tell them that I had come out alive from the hell, but I hung up before I could speak in the phone. Even if in public holiday gathering between relatives, everyone is very good at tacit cooperation, and they avoid talking about my case, it just feels like air! It seems that the environment and society around me have completely stopped accepting me back to normal.

The person most affected by the unjust case was my mother XIN Hong. I was once her proud son! On the unfamiliar streets and darkest day of 'total solar eclipse' in Hangzhou, Zhejiang Province, the Chaozhou police from Guangdong Province arrested me in front of her with the full cooperation of the local Hangzhou police. In the past eight years (2009-2017), I don't know how she survived day by day as a mother. Faced with the incomprehension and gossip from outsiders, the only one who always stood firmly with me was my mother. Even though the unjust case was overturned, some people around me still joked: No matter how right you were, you got yourself involved in a criminal trap and even got divorced. Isn't this

本书尽可能详尽地记录了儿子郭利在过去
十六年中的历经艰辛，从冤狱到无罪的翻
案过程，揭露了中国司法不公平生的环境与根
源，展现了对其所在成长地的绝望。
预祝本书完稿，翻译与今后的出版发行！

母亲、辛宏
2024年5月19日
北京

My mother XinHong's congratulatory message

to my book <A Flying Dad>

stupid and fool head? You deserve it. After I was released from prison, I had no source of income and relied on my brother's support and my mother's pension for several years. During the three years period of looking for evidence and investigating the wrong case, my mother had been running around with me everywhere. Without any social resources or help from my original social connections, only my mother persisted with me for fighting just eight years. To be honest, my mother had a harder time than I did through these long and humiliating huge prison years in China, actually she's in the Great Prison of China.

In the 16 years since the 'melamine-milk' scandal, no one has told the parents what the future holds for their harmed babies with 'kidney-stones'. Even if the verdict like mine is acquitted, it will not be the end of rights defending, but it will return to the point of restart.

Since Guangdong Provincial High Court has acquitted me, the people who reported the false case and their 'evil forces' who framed me and their companies like Yashily & Scient must be guilty and have the nature of false accusations and frame-ups. The original first-instance, second-instance and 1st retrial case-handling authorities and their responsible persons were also guilty and at fault. During eight years that I was wrongfully imprisoned and appealed to 2nd retrial, COFCO Mengniu*Yashily Int'l and its "money-laundry" agent Zhang Litian's family has been taking advantage of his "white gloves" companies（白手套企业）and high-level background in government, business and enterprise connections with Beijing, and after cashing out nearly 5.8 billion Yuan (~USD 828,571,000) in Hong Kong stock market in 2013, he continued to collude with the Guangdong judiciary and his "protective umbrella" in the central party（中央保护伞）in Beijing to deal with me and the lawyers or citizen agents who wanted to help me (such as Sally Zhu, Tina Zhang & Zhonghua Deng, etc.). For this reason, in the following month after the case was overturned, my mother and I walked on our road of cross-provincial accusation and full disclosure of rights defense.

In order to save money, we usually have to take a green (very old and slow) train or a hard sleeper from Beijing to Guangdong to report the case to the local police, and hold the criminal accountability of Yashily's senior executives who participated in the framing of my wrongful case. We went to Chao'an County (now district), called the police number 110 on the spot many times, entered Xiangqiao Police Branch Station of Chaozhou to report the case orally and in writing, submitted facts and evidence, and waited for them to accept and file the case; Again and again, we personally traveled thousands of miles to the scene of the incident. We also went to Chaozhou, going back and forth to the City Police Bureau, the Procuratorate, and the district court, along with our non-stop rush and long waits. For an unjust case that should not have

Guo, Li standing in front of a Courthouse in Chaozhou, Guangdong

happened, or even if it had just happened, it would have been enough time for the judiciary to correct the mistake by the end of 2009, but it was covered up and delayed by the Yashily, the "evil forces" in collusion with the local Government Official businesses or GuanShang(官商 in Chinese) and it had been delayed for eight years. Looking at the results of the revised 2nd retrial sentence, it was only a partial revision. The Guo, Li's "crime" of extortion was corrected, but Yashily's crime of false accusation and frame-up was not pursued, and in the end, my civil claim against them was not reflected in it.

Obviously, after the verdict was reversed in 2017, a long long road to defending my own rights has just begun!

# Chapter 6.

## Continuing to defend legitimate rights, sued for compensations and a full state compensation package

From being released from prison at the end of my five year sentence to successfully overturning the case, this journey took me nearly three years. According to the document of (2015) YueGaoFaShengXingJianZaiZi No. 19 Judgment issued by Guangdong Provincial High Court on April 7th 2017, in accordance with the State Compensation Law of the People's Republic of China, I can apply for state compensations from the various authorities responsible for compensation involved in the case "within two years after being acquitted". After obtaining the final judgment of 2nd retrial, I launched an investigation in accordance with the Chinese criminal law for their crime of falsely accusing and framing me by Yashily & Scient Companies and its Chairman Zhang Litian. At the same time, the road to my compensation for the state ones has also been officially launched accordingly.

In addition to Zhang Yansheng and Gongsun Xue, who were hired by my family of the original first instance, as the lawyers for my case, the following original second instance, the 1st retrial of the Intermediate Court and the 2nd retrial of the High Court can really be said to have "no help from the agency or lawyer's profession"! When Chaozhou Intermediate Court in Guangdong Province convicted me and sentenced me to five years in prison, I appeared in court alone, and there was no one in the audience seats behind me, except for the people from the "Yashily & Scient" (Nicknamed as Evil Forces in Chinese) police, Procuratorate and law courts. Without an effective agent or lawyer, only by entirely relying on myself and the persistence of my mother who is remotely living in Beijing can this unjust case be successfully overturned. For quite some time after the acquittal was commuted, Chinese law firms, the lawyers and medias from all over the country swarmed in. The scene was very lively. The emergence of this kind of human environment made me feel mixed emotions. I sincerely feel that this world no longer provides help when needed, but more icing on the cake or their purpose is just to rub the heat.

After my success, some well-known law firms and lawyers threw olive branches to me and my family, and expressed their intention to represent me in the "State Compensation" series of cases after my acquittal. One of them is Beijing Huayi Law

Guo, Li, Pu Zhiqiang, and Qu Zhenhong,

in Hua Yi Lawyer's office, Beijing

Firm, which is very famous for helping injured or harmed parts apply for state compensation and representing some Chinese sensitive cases. Mr. LUO Xiang, China's most famous law professor, is also a lawyer at the firm.

Qu Zhenhong, the director of the law firm, and Pu Zhiqiang, a former lawyer and leader of the 1989-June-4th Chinese student movement, personally received us and expressed their willingness to represent me in the state compensation case. During the meeting, Qu, the director of the law firm, stressed to me that she and Pu had also been in prison and were therefore "qualified" to represent me in my case. Because I used to say that "in China, a lawyer who has not been in prison will not be a real lawyer......". They also made remarks about "bizarre theories" that wanted me to have a higher political consciousness and go in the "correct" direction of the country's justice. However these are contrary to my original intention (initiation) of firmly and thoroughly investigating and defending my legitimate rights!

I am determined to defend my rights. Firstly, in order to thoroughly expose the truth through my own real events, in order to obtain the fairness and justice of real state compensation cases; Secondly, in order to safeguard the legitimate rights and interests of tens of millions of victimized consumers and their families in accordance with the law, and to ensure food safety and maintain a green environment to the

罗翔，1977年出生，湖南耒阳人

中国政法大学刑事司法学院教授

罗老师他"说的就是你"：
@斗士力郭 DareDream
南征北战08-22

勇敢
在我的词典里
是一个最高级的词汇…

Chinese famous law professor, jurist and lawyer, Luo, Xiang

greatest extent; Thirdly, to promote real progress in China's judicial fairness and human rights; It is not for the sake of being subordinate to today's elite, kneeling and licking and acknowledging or praising and singing praises, and it has nothing to do with its so-called political consciousness and other factors. After meeting and making further trade-offs, we rejected the agency intention of Beijing Huayi Law Firm, and finally chose to continue with our mother XIN Hong and a few like-minded friends.

Since I have no source of income after being released

from prison, the biggest problem is to raise enough funds for rights defending activity and arranging domestic travel. At first, I took the most economical coach train by myself, riding from Beijing West Railway Station to Guangzhou Railway Station, and then from Guangzhou East Railway Station to ChaoShan Station, during which I arranged to visit Chaozhou, Chao'an and Jieyang areas on the same day in order to save the costs, and tried to finish our work in one day, and then returned to the most important point of the cities.

After the medical diagnosis confirmed that I had a physical disability and could not bear weight, I asked my mother to follow and start running around for the sake of safety and evidence collection issues. She was in her 70s at the time, and she was unable to walk because of a falling down and bone injury. Since the case was reversed in 2017, my mother and I had travelled back and forth between Beijing, Guangdong, Shenzhen and Hong Kong more than 30 times. In the process of handling various affairs, we always plan the itinerary reasonably, and combine the time to meet with authorities and departments at all levels, so as to greatly save our travel expenses and improve the efficiency of the planned destinations we have to visit. For example, every time we go to Guangdong to do business, we strive to go back and forth to more than three regions within five days a week, and ran between departments at all levels. After finished the court work, we immediately went to the Police Dept. and the Prison

Guo, Li standing in front of a court with the drawing he drew in prison

and paper marked Poison-formula Yashily

Administration to handle relevant legal issues, and if we had enough time left, we would make an arrangement on a Procuratorate visit in between. With such a tight budget & schedule, we have achieved the highest efficiency by using a handful of limited case-handling money.

In the process of evidence collecting at the Chaozhou Court, we have encountered all kinds of clerks, most of whom are perfunctory and arrogant. Every time we asked to copy files of particulars or access disclosure information, they are always arrogant, demanding payment, and even making things difficult. They often deliberately torture us like "squeezing toothpaste", and gave us the incomplete information for several times. There are also individual differences. I once met a female judge in the case registry office, in her 40s, who is also estimated to be the mother of a child. When receiving us, she always explained patiently with a pleasant face and was very amiable; In the process of copying and consulting the files of particulars with her, we were never asked to pay; I think it's probably because she is also a mother. In fact, no mother wants her child to eat unsafe and toxic food that causes harm of the child health. Her admiration and respect for my experiences and tribulations can be seen to be sincere and from the bottom of her heart.

Not long after the case was overturned, several mainstream medias in China conducted an exclusive interview with me. I printed the cover of the interview with me in the News-Week column hosted by Bai Yansong, a famous TV host of China Central Television or CCTV, on a piece of cotton cloth and carefully sewed it onto my hoody.

When I submitted the application for China state compensation, I went straight to the Chaozhou Intermediate Court with the baby formula cans containing the 'poisoned milk powder' and the above-mentioned logo pattern of human rights defender clothes. Because Yashily's Scient claims to be the US brand, some of the materials in my claim are in English. At that time, when the clerk of the case filing registry saw the evidence items that we were still carrying, they got angry at us and asked me to remove the cans and clothes from their office desks. Then, flipping through the application materials we submitted..., they didn't even look at it carefully, so they told us to ask the translation company to have it translated and then resubmit it. I immediately said: I'm the translator. These materials have been translated and provided in both Chinese and English. The clerk asked "Then what are you doing in English?" I replied: This is my civil right!

After five or six such kind of visits, we found that the attitude of the clerks had changed, or that they had been instructed by their superiors. Gradually, I saw that there were smiling faces, from the initial aloof, disrespectful and arrogance, to the later respect, admiration and patience. At my insistence in accordance with the law, the Finance Department of Chaozhou Intermediate Court reimbursed 7,209 Yuan (~USD 1,000) for our travel expenses to and from Beijing to Chaozhou for the state compensation case. The source of this travel expense has also become one of the important claims basis for me to apply for subsequent "State Compensation" series of cases.

After more than half a year of evidence collection, dictation, collation, review and writing, I finally submitted the 256-page "Guo, Li's Application for State Compensation" in paper to the Intermediate Court of Chaozhou, Guangdong Province. In this application, I set out in detail the contents of the victim's application for state compensation, including seven major items of claim, such as my lost work expenses, mental harm & loss expenses, physical harm, injury & disability plus medical treatment expenses, etc., and the total value of compensation claimed in the case was RMB 228,362,462.64 Yuan（~USD 32,623,208.95）.

On December 18th 2017, I got the court case schedule notice from Chaozhou Intermediate Court (2017) Yue51FaPei No. 2. The cause of this case was: [The Compensation Case for Retrial to Change the Verdict to Not Guilty]. The case should be concluded in March 18th 2018. On the same day, a female judge named Chen made an investigation record on my application for state compensation.

At 14:30 p.m. on January 31st 2018, Chaozhou Intermediate Court formed a collegial panel to hear opinions and meet for trial in the compensation case of my 2nd retrial and acquittal. Several leaders of Chaozhou Intermediate Court attended the meeting. In a narrow and closed reception room, a vice president of the Court (note: Deng Xiasi, the former president of Chaozhou Intermediate Court in the compensation part of the court, has been dismissed and sentenced in jail by CCP Guangdong), Zhang Yuebin, the judge in charge of administrative compensation office, and the clerks all appeared. Once again, we express our strong protest and dissatisfaction with the Chaozhou law courts' misjudgment of the case of concocted "extortion" and the consequences thereof. In the reception room, the vice president cowered and quickly shook hands with me without outsiders, and only expressed his private apologies for the court's three time deliberate misjudgments. We are very dissatisfied with such "non-public" action and misconduct!

So far, in my application documents for "State Compensation" and other official comments in the public media,

I have clearly requested compensation from the Chaozhou Police Dept., Detention Center, Procuratorate, Three-level Law courts, Jieyang Prison and other government depts. involved in the case must "openly and formally" apologize to the victims for concocting Guo Li's unjust, false and wrongly decided case. When I signed the transcript after listening to the opinions, I said to the vice president of Chaozhou Intermediate Court, who participated in this meeting: I have walked for eight years on the road of seeking state compensation; I hope that the road of my rights defending will not require me to go for another eight years.

On February 21st 2018, I received the document of (2017) Yue51FaPei No. 2 State Compensation Decision from

Guo, Li in the meeting with judge of Guangdong

Chaozhou Intermediate People's Court of Guangdong Province by mail in Beijing. Once again, I am very disappointed and regretful that they rejected most of the contents of my claim for compensation, and only compensated a little more than RMB 500,000 yuan for my lost work expenses and a little more than RMB 100,000 yuan for my mental harm or damages in accordance with China's national average wage standard for workers or employees, totaling around RMB 640,000 yuan （~USD 91,428.60）.

The content of Chaozhou Intermediate Court's decision is undoubtedly very different from my actual losses, damages and expectations. For this reason, it is inevitable to lodge a reconsideration of the above-mentioned no award of compensation issue with Guangdong Provincial High Court, the superior court.

The various evidentiary aspects of my state compensation claim process are fraught with difficulties. For example, when Beijing Xuanwu Hospital, where I was diagnosed and treated, wanted to issue me a certificate of diagnosis of injury or illness, they are notified that the relevant medical departments and hospital director office all stipulated that the public security dept. where the person's (injured or sickened patient) household registration was located or the prison where the person was originally detained could issue an official letter of introduction before the person (the patient) concerned could be issued with a valid diagnosis document. In short, the certificate can't be issued to me, so this also delays and wastes my time. After I was retried and acquitted, the above-mentioned hospitals were forced to issue me post-diagnosis certificates for various disciplines due to a part of reasons that I might expose to the medias and trigger public pressure.

Jieyang Prison and Chaozhou Intermediate Court in Guangdong Province, which are also one of the authorities obligated to pay the state compensations, also refused to admit that my physical and mental disabilities were caused by ill-treatment, torture, starvation and beatings during my unjust imprisonment. They claim that they are not the legally liable authorities under the Law on State Compensation. On the contrary, Jieyang Prison also argued that the wrongful judgment of Chaozhou Intermediate Court led to the wrongful detention of the victim Guo, Li, saying that the responsibility for disabling Guo, Li's body and mind was not in prison, and therefore it believed that Jieyang Prison should not be the authority of the state obligation to compensate. Chaozhou Intermediate Court of Guangdong Province retaliated with this, saying that the victim Guo, Li could not provide evidence to prove that Chaozhou Intermediate Court's guilty verdict had infringed on his right to life and health, and that Guo, Li believed that he had been ill-treated, handcuffed and shackled, and fasted from drinking and eating in jails, and that Guo, Li, he could find another legal way to resolve it.

After Chaozhou Intermediate Court of Guangdong Province told me to "seek another legal way to solve" the issue of compensations, and I sought to resolve and pursue it in accordance with the Chinese law, Jieyang Prison in Guangdong Province claimed that it was because of the wrong judgment of the Law court that caused my disability and illness. They do not abide by the law, and they can only pass the buck to each other and shirk the responsibility of the state, which is the authority obligated to make compensation. And to whom should I, as an injured and harmed part, sue, assert and claim for my legitimate rights and interests? Where can the legal remedies for my state compensation be obtained and reflected? In addition, I asked the above-mentioned authorities to make a public apology, and Jieyang Prison and the Chaozhou court gave us the same answer, insisting that the matter was not their business and refusing to publicly apologize to the victim and his family.

Due to the complex background and huge political impact of the 'melamine-milk' exposure incident, the move of the "Guo, Li's State Compensation Case" that I applied for has also attracted much attention and has been monitored and maintained by the whole 'WeiWen' system (Maintain Stability by Using Unlawful Judicial Forces) in China and even across countries. Because melamine 'baby formula scandal' involves Chinese deep politics, collusion with domestic and foreign capital, and touches on sensitive issues of people's livelihood, the impact is HUGE. After I was arrested across the province for rights defending, Yashily International Group was listed publicly in Hong Kong stock market during the collusion between politics and business, and soon after the mediation of the Chinese Ministry of Agriculture and the auspices and care of former Vice Premier Zhang Dejiang and Wang Yang, it was quickly acquired by COFCO Mengniu Group, which is a major central government enterprise, for more than 10 billion yuan (~USD 1,428,571,429 or ~HKD11,000,000,000 ). Zhang Litian, the former Chair of Yashily International, is also a key delegate to the National People's Congress for Guangdong Province. After I was arrested and imprisoned, the Beijing law firm and its lawyer hired by my family were investigated and threatened by the Chinese Ministry of Justice. The then Minister of Justice

Yashily's boss, Zhang Litian, as one delegate to the National People's Congress for Guangdong Province, standing with the Chairman of the Standing Committee, NPC, and Vice Premier of the State Council, PRC, in news report (from NF Daily)

Ms. Wu Aiying also gave Zhang Litian and Yashily full support. Obviously, it is much more challenging and difficult to defend my rights than other normal cases!

I have said the important thing three times: my case has gone through the procedures of the first instance of Chao'an County Court, the second instance and 1st retrial of Chaozhou Intermediate Court, and the 2nd retrial and arraignment of Guangdong Provincial Court; It is a rare case in Chinese modern history that after eight years of "four law court trials", the final judgment from finding the consumer guilty to changing my acquittal. That is to say, this case itself is much more complicated than other normal ordinary criminal cases, and involves many people, stakeholders and departments. Therefore, in the process of subsequent claims and rights defending activity in accordance with the Chinese law, we will naturally have more issues related to the authorities involved in the compensation obligation and the compensation items or objects. Based on this, it is inevitable that the various authorities with the obligation to compensate will inevitably pass the buck and shield each other. Through the legal procedures and process of applying to Chaozhou Intermediate Court for "Guo, Li's State Compensation", we continued to explore, study and learn. And in the claim time, which took more than a year, we submitted the claim materials to different authorities and departments of Guangdong Provincial Public Security Dept., Detention Center, Procuratorate, and Law courts. Ironically, almost every authority and department replied in a surprisingly general way: they are NOT the parts of the obligation to pay compensation to the victim!

After summarizing and analyzing, I found that the situations I encountered were all dealt with by them with endless prevarication and artificially created cumbersome procedures. If we follow the procedures for prosecution one by one, not only will we fail to achieve the goal of pursuing the case, but we will be led by the judiciary and exhaust our limited

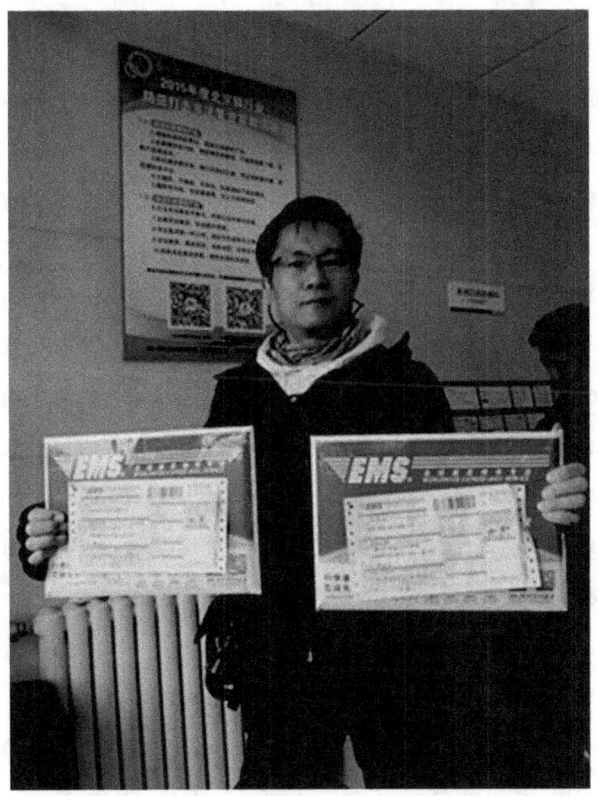

Guo, Li showed the couriers he tried to send to government

departments

financial resources and energy. After re-adjusting our thinking and planning the response measures, almost on the same day and at the same time, we filed a lawsuit against the state compensation or resorted to the court together with the Chao'an County (District) Police and Detention Center of Guangdong Province, the Chaozhou Police and Detention Center, the Chao'an County (District) Court, the Chaozhou Intermediate Court, the Guangdong Provincial Prison Administration and Jieyang Prison, and the latest Guangdong Provincial High Court.

The fact that so many judicial authorities have been sued and prosecuted at the same time is rare for similar state compensation cases after my acquittal has been commuted, and it is also a precedent issue in China. This move has undoubtedly disrupted the unified response steps between these authorities or departments, resulting in contradictions and loopholes between the defenses and evidence in their respective judicial documents in the subsequent response process, and then exposing many flaws and misguidances.

Because of the huge gap between the original compensation decision and my compensation application, and the need to collect, confirm and copy a large number of defense and evidence materials derived from the previous case file, again we went to the Chaozhou Procuratorate, Chaozhou Intermediate Court, Chao'an County (District) Court, Chao'an County (District) Police Station and other authorities to check the files and confirm the relevant contents. During the period of review, confirmation and cross-examination, in order to shirk their respective statutory obligations of compensation, the above-mentioned judicial authorities exposed many bizarre and strange things, For example: previously, the police clearly provided us with a copied "List of Seized Personal Items". But in the Court session, such legal existence of the document was "flatly denied" during the court cross-examination procedure conducted by the Guangdong Provincial High Court.

In nearly three years between my releasing from prison and my acquittal, although my accusations and claims were premised on my innocence, my technical approach was to prepare at the same time. However, the claims on the grounds of innocence have been met with unreasonable shirking of responsibility for the obligation of compensation that should have been borne by various levels of authorities. In the course of the defending, all that arose was the deliberate deception of the indemnity obligated authorities and the partiality of the trial court, as well as their almost predictable, ridiculous and shameful performance.

After being released from prison, I was diagnosed with a variety of chronic diseases after several medical examinations and diagnoses. Diabetes is usually understood to be caused by the accumulation of excess nutrients in the human body. However, I was starved for a long time in prison, malnourished, and mentally compulsively stressed. The severity of the severe discomfort in my lower back, swelling of my legs and feet, and the convulsions, cramping, spasms at night after being beaten in jails are beyond people's imagination! A medical diagnosis reported that I had a moderate gastric ulcer in my stomach and a traumatic fracture of my lumbar spine. Similar to the injuries and illnesses caused by serving my sentence, in the later claim for "Guo, Li's State Compensation Case" (prison part), Jieyang Prison in Guangdong Province gave us a very strange official explanation.

For example, they first denied that I had been beaten and abused in Jieyang Prison under the Ministry of Justice, said that my injury was from Chaozhou Detention Center under the Ministry of Public Security. Secondly, they denied that the prison restricted my diet and caused me suffering from hunger all year round, said that my diabetes was caused by my preference for high-sugar foods in jails. These bizarre official justifications are grossly inconsistent with the actual circumstances in prison. In addition, Jieyang Prison insisted that I had been injured before I was imprisoned from the police detention center, but in the "Prisoner Health Examination Form" issued by Jieyang Prison itself, it stated that the physical condition of the criminal Guo, Li was good and healthy. At the same time, Jieyang Prison also said in the paper that I had external injuries (lumbar spine) when I was imprisoned from the Police Detention Center. In fact, they confessed that I had been tortured to extract a confession, had been beaten and abused by the detention authority of Guangdong.

Similar justifications also reflect the illegal acts of the

Ministry of Public Security Detention Center and the Ministry of Justice Prison in passing the buck and protecting each other. Jieyang Prison has repeatedly denied that I was restricted and controlled from eating, and stated in the document of "A Reply to Guo, Li's Relevant Issues While Serving His Sentence in JieYang Prison" that Guo, Li's language skills and behavior were not obviously abnormal during his sentence, and he was able to participate in the labor-work arranged by the prison normally. In response to our request about being abused and held in solitary confinement, Jieyang Prison said that because Guo, Li had insisted that he was innocent since he was imprisoned, he refused to participate in the labor activities in prison. However, such a reply shows inconsistencies, inconsistent preambles, confusing logic, and extreme absurdity. I refused to plead guilty nor participate in labor work in the prison, so I was strictly controlled by the prison authority and banned from shopping food in jail. It can be clearly seen from the convict's shopping list records that I cannot be rewarded with extra meals like other inmates in my daily life in prison, and I cannot buy daily groceries and nutritional products according to the regulations of Chinese Prison Law. Five years of starvation and severe malnutrition were solved by my own strong will or by buying sugar, biscuits and pickles. The prisoners' personal belongings and money were also seized and illegally embezzled by the Finance Department of Jieyang Prison. In the process of remediating and making false certificates after the fact, the financial departments of the police detention center and the judicial prison have exposed their infallibility. As a result, Jieyang Prison destroyed the records of prisoners' spending money in their accounting

潮州市潮安区人民法院

告知书

郭利：

关于你 2019 年 9 月 2 日来电要求拷贝（2009）安刑初字第 492 号全部案卷的需求问题告知如下：

根据最高人民法院办公厅《关于案件当事人及其代理人查阅诉讼档案有关问题的复函》（法办[2005]415 号）："按照《人民法院档案管理办法》和《最高人民法院关于诉讼代理人查阅民事案件材料的规定》（法释[2002] 39 号）的规定，当事人也可以查阅刑事案件、行政案件和国家赔偿案件的正卷。" 你作为本案被告人符合上述条件，因而你可查阅、复制我院（2009）安刑初字第 492 号刑事案件审判卷正卷。对于你提出复制检察卷、公安卷的要求，我院没有权力向你提供。

特此告知

潮州市潮安区人民法院办公室
2019 年 9 月 日

Reply from Chao'an Court for Guo, Li's requirement on copying

particular issue for his state compensation package

books in advance, but it still didn't help, and it was exposed by my side, the claimant in accordance with the law at this moment.

In order to prevent me from further revealing the truth, in September 2019, when we went to the Chao'an County (District) Court to copy part of the "lost" file of this case, the court again refused to copy it for us in accordance with the law, and they also issued me a special notice. In fact, in the five years between my releasing from prison and the claim for state compensation, I have required to reproduce it many times in accordance with the law. Did the previous copying behavior of me involve "violations of laws and regulations" by Chao'an County (District) Court?

On July 23rd 2018, Guangdong Provincial High Court established a collegial panel on my claim application and cross-examined me and representatives of Chaozhou Intermediate Court, one of the obligated parts responsible for Guo, Li's state compensations.

During the cross-examination session, we gave detailed explanations and attached evidence materials for each compensation item in the application for the High Court's reconsideration.

The 1st item is on the issue of compensation for the earning I lost in the days I was in jail. At that time, Chaozhou Intermediate Court made a decision to pay around 500,000 yuan (~USD 71,428.57) in compensation according to the state uniform wage standard for workers and employees by simply multiplying the number of days I was detained for five years. We set out in detail the average salary level of employees in Beijing from 2009 to 2018, as well as my previous income from a job as international simultaneous interpreter. It was clearly pointed out that Chaozhou

Guo, Li standing in front of the Chao'an Court in Chaozhou,

Guangdong

Intermediate Court did not take into account the actual situation of the victim's work and life standard in Beijing in accordance with the law, and adopted this unified standard (which is actually the minimum state wage/pay standard) to calculate my compensation, which is very wrong and extremely irresponsible.

The 2nd item is on the issue of claims for travel expenses. Chaozhou Intermediate Court argued that there was no explicit legal provision in the law on compensation for the travel expenses of the victim part. Based on my wrongful judgment, the court used to reimburse me as victim for 7,209 yuan (~USD 1,000) for travel expenses under the "special" care they gave me within the scope of their subsidy. On the other hand, we relied on the wrongly judged subject of compensation to be Chaozhou Intermediate Court.

We believe that the one who is responsible for my wrongful conviction is Chaozhou Intermediate Court. If it were not for the court's wrongful judgment, these travel expenses would not be our necessary expenses. Therefore, the travel expenses that should not have been borne by me should be borne by the obligated authority responsible for the wrongful conviction.

The 3rd item is on the issue of public apologies. Referring to the well-known 'Nie Shubin' (an innocent person was wrongly sentenced to death) case in China at that time, I, the part of victim, demanded that Chaozhou Intermediate Court must make a formal and sincere apology to the victim on the Internet, media and other public occasions. Chaozhou Intermediate Court, on the other hand, argued that it had apologized to me privately in accepting my application for compensation. For this reason, my mother XIN Hong, also made a special explanation to the Provincial High Court on this matter. After I was released from prison, I was able to see my child on holidays. But after the case was successfully overturned, the media publicly reported on my incident, and the child learned about me through the online media, and she knew that her father had disappeared and was kept in prison for five years. At that time, my child was just 12 years old, and she still couldn't understand what happened to me. What she knew at once was that her father as "A Flying Dad" turned out to be a prisoner, a convicted inmate in Guangdong. The classmates around her who knew this all laughed at her, and she found it difficult to accept the fact and felt it's a great shame. Ever since then, she found out, then she won't and hasn't seen me again. Based on this reality, we insist that the Chaozhou Intermediate Court should make a public and formal apology to me in accordance with the law in the form of referring to the "Nie Shubin" case. The fact that Chaozhou Intermediate Court has taken the action of apologizing in private is not sincere for correcting its mistakes and has no significance in judicial education of China.

The 4th item is on the issue of applying for the child's later medical treatment and child support payment. I asked the child's current caregiver to make a detailed list on medical records. Melamine in baby formula damage on children's body is irreversible for life. The child was accompanied by frequent dizziness, inability to attend physical education classes in schools, and sequelae such as epilepsy etc. However, because I was unjustly imprisoned for five years, I failed to fulfill my legal guardian obligation to support the child, and I lost my ability to support her in the future due to disability and illness caused by the prison. According to the Chinese State Compensation Law, the authority with the obligation to compensate the injured and harmed part should compensate the direct descendant of the injured and harmed one in accordance with the law. The Chaozhou Intermediate Court completely rejected this claim for compensation, which has no basis in law.

The 5th item is on the issue of claims for my physical disability and illness while in prison. For this reason, we launched a fierce confrontation with Chaozhou Intermediate Court and Jieyang Prison in Guangdong Province. The Chaozhou Intermediate Court held that my disability was caused by Chaozhou Public Security Dept. (Police) and Jieyang Prison under the Ministry of Justice, which were in charge of criminals' detention, and had nothing to do with the law courts, so the Intermediate Court was not an authority obligated to compensate the victim. At the same time, when I was found to be physically disabled after I was released from prison, the Chaozhou Police authority believed that before I was escorted to Jieyang Prison to serve my sentence, I was in 'good' physical condition and had no disability or illness. The disability or illness has nothing to do with the Police under the Ministry of Public Security, and they are not the authority obligated to pay compensation to me as well. Jieyang Prison, on the other hand, argued that the miscarriage of the verdict was caused by the law court, and that they only carried out the erroneous judgment of the law court; The detention and prison authorities flatly denied the evidence we adduced that I was beaten by the police and bandits in collusion and tortured and ill-treated in the prison. However, in the corresponding defense procedure, because we adopted the strategy of a "cluster" type of claims and an unified case filings at the same time, we did not allow them to have the time to reach a consensus and the possibility of mutual cooperation, resulting in a "slap in the face" situation in which the defense and evidence issued by the obligated authorities of state compensations were obviously contradictory and conflicting with each other.

At the same time, we provided a number of evidence and counter-references to the torture of my confession, the beating and maiming of my cell-mates, and the incommunicado management and ill-treatment in custody. These circumstances are supported by early case files and interrogation records. In the original records of interrogation by the former Chao'an County Police, the County Procuratorate, the Chaozhou Intermediate Court, and other case-handling authorities, there were all mentions of torture to extract confessions, threats, not being allowed to sleep for several days and nights, being held alone with restraints, and being beaten by other detainees in the detention center. We have corresponding original records, witness testimony and other supporting evidence. A year before I was released from prison in 2014, I was held in solitary confinement in Jieyang Prison in the inmate hospital area after being physically disabled. During this period, I applied to the head of the prison section to make a family phone call, and the prison district also gave a written reply on this. This original written application and reply documents also confirms that I was in sick condition and badly treated in prison.

After I was released from prison, several AAA-rated hospitals in Beijing also gave me a multidisciplinary medical evaluation of my health condition and disability, which was enough to prove that my disability was caused by five years of unjust imprisonment. Chaozhou Intermediate Court held that my disability was not caused by them, but it could not produce evidence to substantiate it. It can only be argued that we need to prove that the disability and illness were caused in prison. In fact, it becomes a question of putting the cart before the horse. The fact that the state law requires that whoever asserts the claim should provide evidence, but the law court made such an illegal request to the victim, which is a typical manifestation of the law enforcement's knowledge of the law and resistance to the law.

They repeatedly struggled with the two 'technical' terms of rights of personal life and rights of health. There are many contradictions in the defense. For example, Jieyang Prison recorded in its prison sentence assessment that Guo basically did not participate in productive labor-work during his sentence, did not plead guilty to the law, performed poorly in thought changing, and did not receive any administrative reward. Guo did not meet the relevant conditions for commutation and parole, so there is no commutation of the sentence during his imprisonment. In another disability claim case of mine, the "Reply Letter Concerning Guo, Li's Situation During His Sentence" issued by Jieyang Prison to Chaozhou Intermediate Court also stated: While serving his sentence, Guo, Li's language and behavior showed no obvious abnormalities. He can participate in the labor-work arranged by the prison normally. Regarding the issue of Guo being disabled, Jieyang Prison stated that I was in good physical condition and had no health abnormality in prison, while Chaozhou Police Detention Center stated: Guo was the focus of the sick inmates in his 1st retrial session when he was escorted from Jieyang Prison back to Chaozhou Detention Center. Similar and inconsistent defenses abound in the multiple state compensation claims we filed simultaneously.

Another very important part of the application for my state compensation is to investigate the issue of Zhang Litian, Wu Xiaonan and others of Yashily International Group who falsely accused and framed me. So far, Chaozhou Public Security Dept. of Guangdong Province has not filed a case and prosecuted Zhang Litian, Wu Xiaonan, and others for falsely accusing and framing Guo, Li of their criminal acts in accordance with the Chinese Criminal Law. Even Guangdong local authorities have vigorously protected their Yashily culpability. This is also the best case-study and example of collusion between the government and 'GuanShang' business (or The Government Officials' dealing with the Businessman). It is also my case that has caused the world to feel in an uproar, jaw-dropping and intriguing, showing the shady scenes of judicial corruption in China.

In the end, Guangdong Provincial High Court, one of the obligated authorities that heard Guo, Li's compensation case,

2. 据郭利提供的材料，其在 2017 年 6 月至 2018 年 6 月期间到首都医科大学宣武医院等医院就诊及检查，结果为双眼视物模糊、脑血管病（慢性病）和动脉硬化、脂肪肝等。

3. 据揭阳监狱《关于郭利在服刑期间有关情况的复函》，郭利在服刑期间，语言和行为未见明显异常，能正常参加监狱安排的劳动；郭利因疑似 "糖尿病" 在监狱医院留院观察十天，经检查身体未见明显异常；因腰痛、咳嗽、支气管炎等疾病多次在监狱医院门诊治疗；驻监检察机关没有郭利在服刑期间被殴打、虐待情况的投诉记录。

Files retrieved from the court for Guo's harmed and injuries issues by police and prison administration in Guangdong, China asked us if there was any supplement to our state compensation claim application, and we said that we would add 5 million yuan ( ~USD 714,286 ). The Court also asked us if we agreed to mediation, and we said yes. Zhang Yuebin, a representative of Chaozhou Intermediate Court, said that they needed to report to their boss after returning to the Chaozhou city and discuss a reply.

In addition to applying for state compensation, we also filed an administrative lawsuit against the public security dept. (police) in Chaozhou City, Guangdong Province, regarding the loss of personal belongings at my home in Beijing. It is not difficult to predict that the local authorities involved in the case have passed the buck and protected each other, and their rhetoric is contradictory. The complete chain of facts and evidence related to this case has been recorded by our side. Regarding the claim for the illegal seizure of Guo, Li's personal belongings by Chao'an County (District) Police, we has the document of "seizure list" issued from former Chao'an County Public Security Dept. Later, the police found that the procedures and content of the case involving their personnel were illegal, the document as an evidence was then destroyed or hidden. However, before their destruction, we actually used legal means to have a copy of it in the early stage from Chao'an County Court of the original trial.

Referring to this incident, I recall that on July 23rd, 2014, almost at the same time as the inter-provincial police team arresting me in Hangzhou of Zhejiang Province, another special group of police from Guangdong, together with my ex-wife's best friend Zhang Lin, raided my residence place in Xicheng District in Beijing. In the process of raiding, the police illegally seized some samples of Scient baby formula in the room, and also stole my personal collection of philatelic albums, Lamborghini racing suits and other precious items, which were not recorded in the Seizure List, registered and kept in accordance with the Chinese Criminal Procedure Law, and were later missing! On the police Seizure list, my ex-wife GaoHong had signed the possession of the items, but she did not obtain the original signature copy of the list that should have been provided by the case-handling polices at present. The real owner of these items is me, and the police raiding and items seized list should be signed by me, instead of her. However, in the 'Witnesses' column on the items seized list, Zhang Lin's signature appears, she is one of the conspirators involved in Yashily's concoction of the unjust case, and it is obviously illegal for her to sign as a witness. As a result, the evidence of the [Seizure] list that we obtained from the original trial court was full of illegal processing and information.

As one of the core pieces of evidence in the 2nd state compensation case, when I submitted my claim to the court, the judge in the reconsideration procedure specifically verified this request. The judge also made an annotation on the copy of the [Seizure] list submitted by our side: "After Chaozhou Intermediate People's Court went to Chao'an County Court to check the criminal file, the (Chaozhou police) public security did not transfer this seizure list." With regard to the list of claims for illegal seizure of personal belongings of Guo, Li, the Intermediate People's Court of Chaozhou of Guangdong Province, argued that since there was no record of the [Seizure]

Screenshots from famous law professor Luo, Xiang's public speech, which talking about Guo, Li's case as an example in law practice for Law Certificate Examination

list from the police, it was impossible to judge the loss of personal belongings, and therefore the evidence can't support Guo, Li's claim for state compensation for this item. However, they deliberately forgot that this list of evidence had been

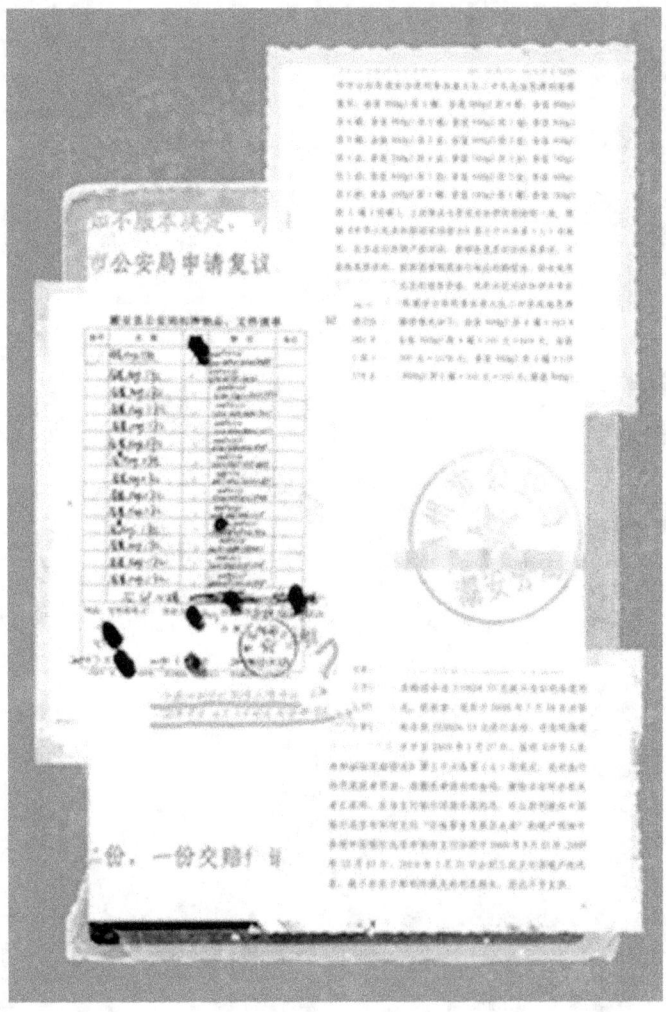

Records of police violation against laws in Guo's wrongful state compensation package

copied within a year of my unjust release from the Jieyang prison. In front of the evidence, they were dumbfounded and confused. Therefore, in desperation, the Chaozhou court made

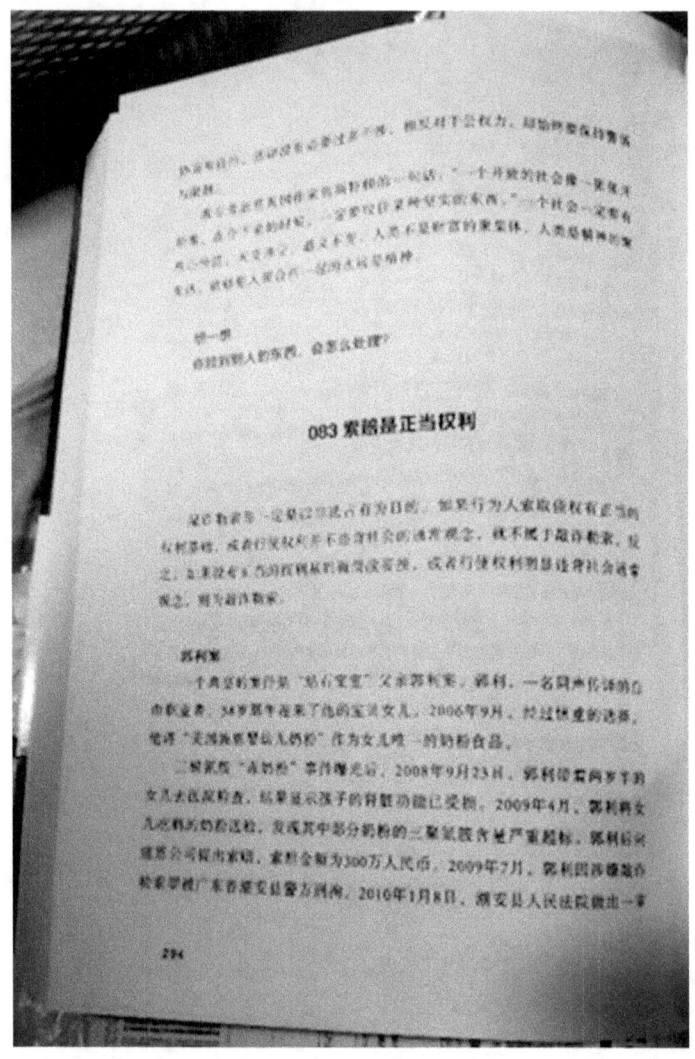

Some legal definition and Guo, Li's case as an example

in Luo, Xiang's textbook about Chinese Criminal law cases

another one, which is my 2nd compensation judgment of RMB 5,690.30 Yuan (~USD 812.90) in the case of "Guo, Li's State Compensation(s)" for the loss of personal belongings seized by the polices raiding in my home. Through the content of the judgment and the defense of the defendant and the law court, the collusion, cover-up and deception of the judicial authorities in the process of my rights defending are thoroughly exposed.

It should be added that when I was arraigned by the judges of the Chaozhou Intermediate Court during the 1st retrial in 2010, I personally reported to them about the beating and ill-treatment in the Chao'An and Jieyang prisons. At the same time, I asked the Court of the original trial that if I was still found guilty in the retrial, please do not send me back to Jieyang Prison to serve my sentence. At that time, the judge said that they had made a record and would promptly reflect my request to the relevant law enforcement departments. However, the Chaozhou Intermediate Court ignored this historical fact and documentary evidence. And the judges, prosecutors, and police officers who were in charge of making my wrong case were also examined or dealt with the CCP punishment accordingly because of my following reports.

The process of defending my legal rights is undoubtedly very different from the current result and the original intention for me. But because of my persistence, my case has had a significant impact on the current process of China's food safety

Front cover of one textbook written by Luo, Xiang about Chinese

Criminal Law

legislation and judicial reform. Big figures in the legal profession, including law professor LUO Xiang, an authority on Chinese criminal law and a well-known jurist, mentioned several times in his open lectures about the China National Law Examination that my case has a direct impact on the clear definition of the crime of extortion and extortion in the field of consumption by the Chinese Supreme Court, the Ministry of Justice, as well as the detailed revision of the supporting provisions of the Chinese Prison Law on the issue of convicts admitting guilt and accepting the law and commutation and parole. Professor LUO Xiang also mentioned in his work "Lectures on Criminal Law" that the "Provisions on Several Issues Concerning the Specific Application of Law in the Handling of Commutation and Parole Cases" adopted by the Supreme Court of China on September 19th 2016 and implemented on January 1st 2018 has a very special provision on the condition of "admission of guilt and repentance" for commutation: "The right of a convict to appeal during the execution of the sentence shall be protected in accordance with the law, and his or her legitimate appeal cannot be regarded as a non-admission of guilt and repentance without analysis." My case is written in the book as a standard example after legal definition on consumer's compensation.

Perhaps I, Mr. Guo, Li, made a significant contribution to this Clause.

From 2008 to 2024, the sixteen years of fighting alone for defending my legal rights, although the pace was extremely difficult and challenging, at the time of the publication of this book in English, the results I expected for years were not seen in China. However, if there is still a man who persists in fighting for this reason, and uses my actions and deeds to promote the reform of China's judiciary and the progress of Chinese rule of law, this is also the original intention from my heart.

After more than three months of preparation, on May 28th 2018, we submitted an application for reconsideration of state compensation to the Guangdong Provincial High Court. On the eve of preparing to go to the Guangdong Provincial High Court in Guangzhou, the provincial capital of Guangdong. I also encountered a strange thing. After Guangdong Provincial High Court mailed the "Notice of Cross-examination" officially issued by the Court office to my address in Beijing, within an hour when the court's special delivery document had arrived in Beijing and had been sorted by the China Post Office in Haidian District of Beijing, within an hour of waiting, the special document was found to have been "disappeared" in the office of the China Post Haidian District!

After repeatedly confirming that the special delivery to me had indeed been lost, we immediately contacted Guangdong Provincial High Court by phone and asked them to resend it and inform us verbally of the specific content of the NOTICE. The judge of the High Court replied that such a practice was inconsistent with the provisions of the law, that is, it was not possible to repeatedly send the same legal documents with the same case number and orally disclose the facts of the case to the parts to the case. After the two sides verified the loss, the China Post Beijing Haidian Office were forced to apologize to me and my family in person, and paid compensation of nearly 10,000 yuan (~USD 1,428.57) for the loss of personal travel, time and work wasting caused by their mistake. On second thought, it is a very strange event that the court's express mail document can be 'lost' in its office. A China Post Internal records indicate that the mail was once present on their post office desk. Whether or not because of some peculiarities of this case that some internal obstacles were arranged to

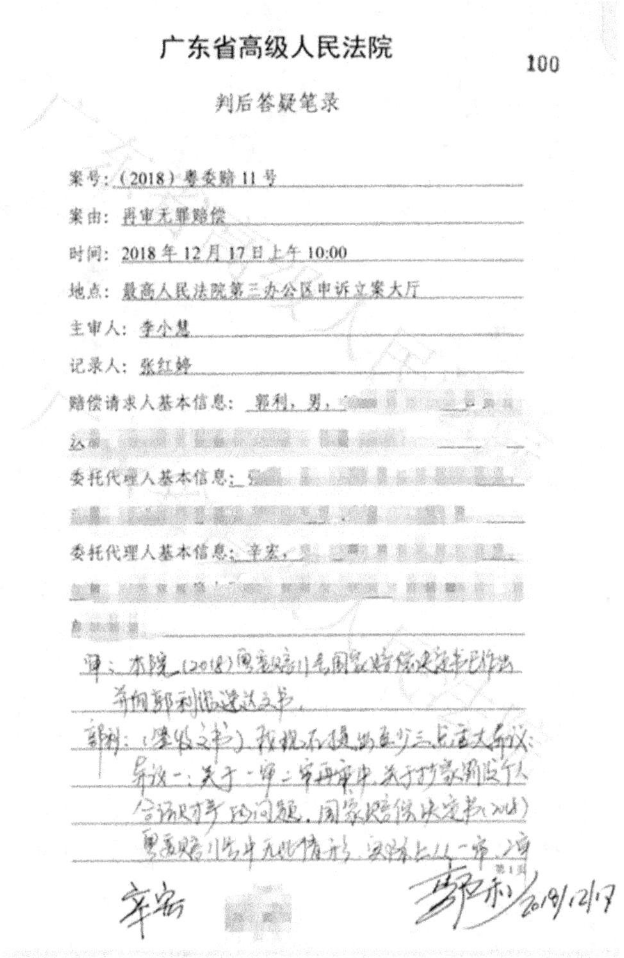

广东省高级人民法院

判后答疑笔录

100

案号：（2018）粤委赔 11 号

案由：再审无罪赔偿

时间：2018 年 12 月 17 日上午 10:00

地点：最高人民法院第三办公区申诉立案大厅

主审人：李小慧

记录人：张红婷

赔偿请求人基本信息：郭利，男，

委托代理人基本信息：

委托代理人基本信息：辛宏，

Record of Q&A for State compensation case of Guo

prevent or interfere with them is not known and remains a mystery even till the day I wrote it down. The way China Post Beijing Haidian Office handled this issue and had a more responsible attitude was something we did not expect. If this can lead to the improvement and progress of the quality of postal services in China, then my efforts and persistence are

Guo's requirement to Scient

for "punishing collusion and return my time" (2008-2019)"

worthwhile and not in vain.

A few days before the cross-examination was about to begin, I rushed from Beijing to the Guangdong Provincial High Court to get the above-mentioned legal documents reissued that had been lost from the Beijing post office. After that, Z.H. Deng, a friend in Guangzhou helped us for booking a hotel next

Judges like Li, Xiaohui and Zhang, Hongting of the High Court
in Guo's case at the Supreme Court office, PRC

to the Court building, then we can wait for the officially

beginning of the statutory court cross-examination procedure. On the afternoon of the day before the cross-examination, a judge from the Guangdong Provincial High Court suddenly called me to inform us that the cross-examination session had been temporarily cancelled! We don't know what's causing this, maybe they're all worried or scared of something! With their ulterior concerns and secrets? To this day, there is no answer and the truth that it deserves.

As a matter of fact, although there is a legal basis for the various claims for state compensation that I have filed against the authorities at all levels with compensation obligations in accordance with the law, they have been basically rejected (and revoked) by Guangdong Provincial High Court without any legal reason. When the Provincial High Court served the [Decision] on us, under normal circumstances, I would have gone to the local court in Guangzhou to collect it and answer questions after the judgment. However, it was extremely unusual that three judges and clerks from the Compensation Office of the Guangdong Provincial High Court, such as Li Xiaohui and Zhang Hongting, deliberately led and misled me to an office in the judges' office of the Supreme Court of China, located on Nanding Road in Fengtai District of Beijing, for several hours of post-judgment Q&A. During this period, they also directly suggested that my part submit a complaint to the Chinese Supreme Court in Beijing for the case of "Guo, Li's State Compensation(s)" right after this.

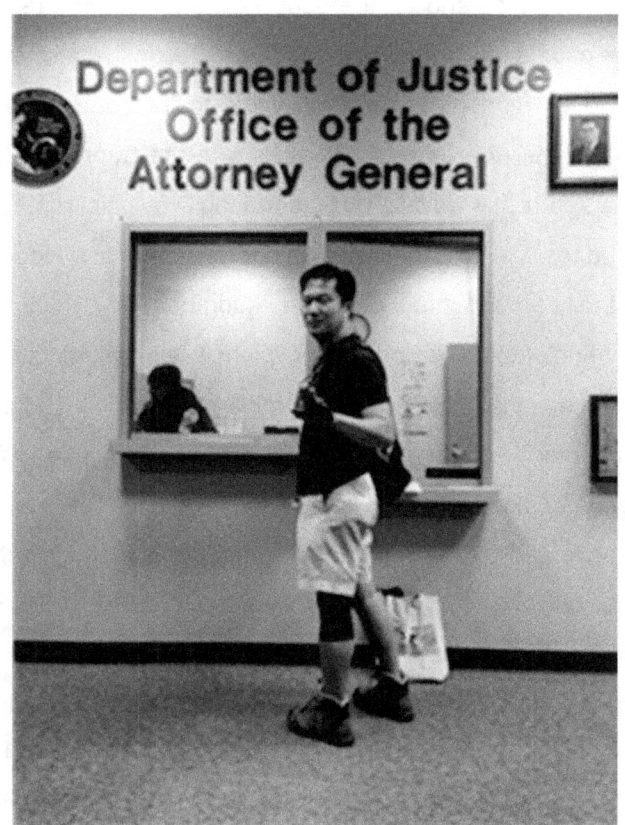

Checking with the US attorney General for the Yashily Scient@Dairy

Brand infringement and counterfeiting issues in China

The problem behind this is that in order to serve a verdict upholding the original verdict, they sent a special representative to meet us in the "judge's office area" of the Chinese Supreme Court. During this period, it was specifically instructed that if I was not satisfied with the decision of the Guangdong Provincial High Court, we could appeal to the Supreme People's Court on the spot. I carefully read the Q&A

after the verdict, and on the spot, I clearly listed the reasons for the court's misjudgment in the "Q&A Record". It also shows that we will find other "correct" ways to file complaints and claims, rather than directly appealing to the Supreme Court, which is currently 'guided' by Guangdong Provincial High Court. The judges handling the case, Li Xiaohui and Zhang Hongting, read the rebuttal content of our post-judgment Q&A documents, and reluctantly affirmed the evidence we submitted and recognized that there were problems in their judgment documents. Soon after, my part filed a separate case to file a "cluster" of application(s) for my state compensation, which was accepted by the relevant Guangdong city or district law courts, but after the case was filed, the content of its (not-) compensation decision was still the same as the previous ones. There are still unreasonable denials of the facts and evidence related to the state compensation owe to the victims, and there is no basis for denying and passing the buck of responsibility for the content of the compensation items such as the injuries, illness and disability caused by the prison to the victim. However, in the face of our solid evidence and facts, it was soon completely exposed and disclosed. In the end, this shows hypocrisy and ugly justice in Guangdong of China.

After supplementation, we submitted a reconsideration letter to the Supreme Court of China on the "Guo, Li State Compensation Case". Soon after, the Supreme Court ruled

Guo in the Church of Bones (The Sedlec Ossuary),

Kutna Hora, the Czech Republic

that it rejected my claim for compensation(s) and the complaint. The reason for this is that our claim for State Compensation has exceeded its statutory two-year statute of limitations. With regard to the two-year statute of limitations, I would like to emphasize here that although my application for compensation was based on the fact that the victim part was acquitted by the court in accordance with the law, and then the case was filed and accepted for compensation in accordance with the State Compensation Law, the case was "suddenly" dismissed on the absurd ground, that is, that the compensation applicant had exceeded the statute of limitations for state compensation prescribed by law. The problem is that the Supreme Court of China, in its judicial interpretation involving this legal provision, issued a new regulation of the State Compensation Law against my claim for state compensation from June 1st 2023:

[Guo, Li's State Compensation Case] AFTER the filed case was "dismissed":

"Interpretation of the Supreme People's Court on Several Issues Concerning the Application of the Statute of Limitation System for Judicial Compensation Cases"

Article 3 If a compensation claimant applies for compensation in accordance with the provisions of Items 4 and 5 of Article 17 of the Chinese State Compensation Law on the grounds that his or her personal rights have been violated, the statute of limitations for the claim shall be calculated from the date when he or she knew or should have known the result of the damage; for damage if the result cannot be determined at that time, the damage shall be calculated from the date the damage result is determined.

Article 4 If a compensation claimant applies for compensation in accordance with Paragraph 1 of Article 18 of the Chinese State Compensation Law on the grounds that property rights have been infringed, the statute of limitations for the claim shall be calculated from the date on which the claimant receives the legal document terminating the criminal proceedings or execution proceedings, but if the case-handling authority has not yet finished disposing of the property involved after the criminal proceedings or execution procedures are concluded, the statute of limitations shall be calculated from the date when the claimant for compensation knew or should have known that his property rights had been infringed.

This interpretation will come into effect on June 1st 2023. After the implementation of this Interpretation, if the case is still under trial, this Interpretation shall apply; if a case in which an effective compensation decision has been made before the implementation of this Interpretation is retried, this Interpretation shall not apply.

[Guo, Li's State Compensation Case] BEFORE the filed case was "dismissed":

According to Article 32 of the "Chinese State Compensation Law": "The statute of limitations for the claimant to request compensation from the authority responsible for compensation is two years, calculated from the date when the behavior of the state authority and its staff when exercising their powers was confirmed to be illegal in accordance with the law, but the period of detention to the claimant is not included. If the claimant is unable to exercise the right to claim due to force majeure or other obstacles within the last 6 months of the statute of limitations for the claim, the statute of limitations shall continue from the date the reason for suspending the statute of limitations is eliminated, calculate."

Accordingly, China's national compensation statute of limitations includes the following:

1. The limitation period is always two years.

2. The statute of limitations for the state compensation is not calculated from the date the victim was harmed, nor from the date the victim knew or should have known that his or her legitimate rights and interests were harmed, rather, it is calculated from the behavior of state authorities and their staff when they exercised their powers to the date on which the violation is confirmed according to law shall be calculated.

A Beijing lawyer called MO Shaoping said in an interview with Radio Free Asia reporter GuTing in the same year: "Legally speaking, if the judicial authority wronged a person and was ultimately found innocent, it should take the initiative to compensate the victim (like Guo, Li) and the person involved!"

Regarding the fact that my appeal was rejected by the Guangdong Provincial High Court and the Supreme Court of China on the grounds that the statute of limitations for compensation had expired, in fact, the response and debate among the legal community was very strong and intense. Most of the well-known scholars and authoritative lawyers in the legal profession are on my side as the victim. They believe that claims for personal injury, harm and property damage should have no statute of limitations, that is, they should be pursued for life. They used real cases as examples, such as the unjust case of 'Nie Shubin' in Hebei Province of China. According to the way the Supreme Court handled my case, Nie's case had already expired, but the Hebei Provincial High Court still issued a public apology and state compensation in accordance with the law to him and his family.

Chinese lawyers generally believe that the court erred in rejecting the victim's application and claim for compensation

China

# Wrongfully jailed father

Guo with other rights-defender's kid

Guo`s visit to.the head office of Mengniu Dairy in Hong Kong

for his compensation issue

on the grounds that the statute of limitations for state compensation has expired. Even in accordance with the relevant provisions of the Chinese State Compensation Law before June 1st 2023, it was mentioned in my 2nd retrial and acquittal that "the victim Guo, Li may claim state compensation within two years after being acquitted in accordance with the Chinese law". But now, the court has illegally rejected my application for state compensation and claim on the grounds that "the statute of limitations of Guo, Li cases has expired", and directly denied the legal rights of the victim and claimant Guo, Li's application for state compensation(s), which the former Guangdong Provincial High Court clearly informed the world when it handed down the not-guilty verdict on April 7th

2017. However, the laws of the country like China can contradict each other, and the reason for refusing to compensate the victim Guo, Li is very shameless and absurd!

Currently, we continue to prepare for the accusation or appeal in the case of "Guo, Li's State (Non) Compensation". Because of my 16 years of fight and perseverance, the Supreme Court, the Supreme Procuratorate and the Ministry of Justice have made amendments and interpretations of a number of legal provisions, including the legislation of the Chinese Food Safety Law. The effective date of the implementation of some of the new laws that have been amended has been implemented immediately after the Guo, Li State Compensation case. Personally, I have not yet enjoyed the same amended genuine human rights and judicial protections that I should have fully enjoyed in accordance with the law. However, because of my persistence and tenacious spirit, I may be

通报：今天双十一，距离何方美（十三妹）被抓捕已经251天了，今天辉县市法院通知我说，本周五开庭审理何方美"寻衅滋事"一案，欢迎亲朋好友前往旁听庭审，让我们一起见证中国法治的进步，...

HE Fangmei with the baby in Henan

able to promote and improve the real progress of China's judiciary and the level of human rights protection issues, so I feel that this is also the greatest significance and courage for me to persist in fighting as a lonely human rights defender.

When it comes to my fellow inmates in Jieyang Prison, I have very little contact, although a few of them have taken the initiative to testify for me; However, the evidence and facts in the dossier of the Guo, Li case are sufficient to explain the legal issues and existence of serious infringement of my personal rights, health rights, and life and property rights.

Actually, I'm not in a hurry to ask my fellow inmates to stand up alone to help testify. On the contrary, some of the inmates and activists from all over China who were crying out for grievances have consulted me on the law and received key guidance in their subsequent personal legal cases because of their various connections with me, such as the family case of LI Xin and HE Fangmei (nick-named the 13th Sister) in Henan Province of China, or because of the influence at home and abroad of my Weibo account Guo-Li@The-Father-of-Kidney-Stone-Babies, and the influence of my reputation in China's human rights defending and legal circles, some of their own issues involving the law have been 'quickly digested' by local civil and judicial authorities, or have been concerned and resolved "under the table" by the case-handling authorities in the place where the case is located, for example: There is a family located near the Lama Temple in Dongcheng District of Beijing, who has been driven away by deliberate noise from a night bar nearby for many years and has been disturbed by life, although this family has insisted on defending their rights for many years but has not made the slightest progress on it. But a few days after I contacted him and spoke out, one day, the night-bar was forced to close due to noise-making issues, and the tort of deliberately interfering with the family's daily life was resolved.

There are also some victims from other places in China who have received help from me or my friends in the process of safeguarding their rights. When the case handling authority or the national security (police) personnel find them and they feel that I and my affairs will cause some pressure or impact on their interests, they will immediately choose to do so. It is shameful and sad to act at the whim of the situation, help in judicial fraud cases and try to frame the helpers of us, such as "The False Accusation Case of TanHua and Her Mother in Shanghai".

Although the "cluster" type of claim process in the case of "Guo, Li's State Compensation(s)" was full of twists and turns, it seems that my compensation application was formally filed and accepted by various compensation authorities and courts in accordance with the Chinese law. But in the end, without exception, they were rejected "according to the law" on the grounds that the local and superior judicial authorities shielded each other, broke the law and negotiated peace, enforced the law and violated the law.

Documents of framing case on the helpers of Guo

in Beijing from Shanghai

In addition to being troubled, interfered with, and obstructed by the China's "Evil Forces" and its public powers, my personal normal life has also been greatly affected. Since 2017, the door lock of my residence in Beijing has been repeatedly blocked by the unknown upstairs residents. After my many complaints and reporting to the police and solemn protests, the Xinjiekou Community Center gave me a separate treatment for installing a new door and replacing the door-lock of my apartment. However in 2019, between my medical treatment in Beijing and my first application for the state compensation package in Guangdong, I found that the tap water in my 1st-floor residence had been completely cut off after the Community Center deliberately re-installed the tap water pipeline underground directly to the 2nd floor and up.

Although we have reported this issue to the Beijing Water Supply Company, XinJieKou Communities Management Company, Xicheng District Government and hotline 12345 for Beijing Municipal Government Citizen Services Beijing for many years, we have not been able to get reasonable compensation and a thorough solution to the problem. And we

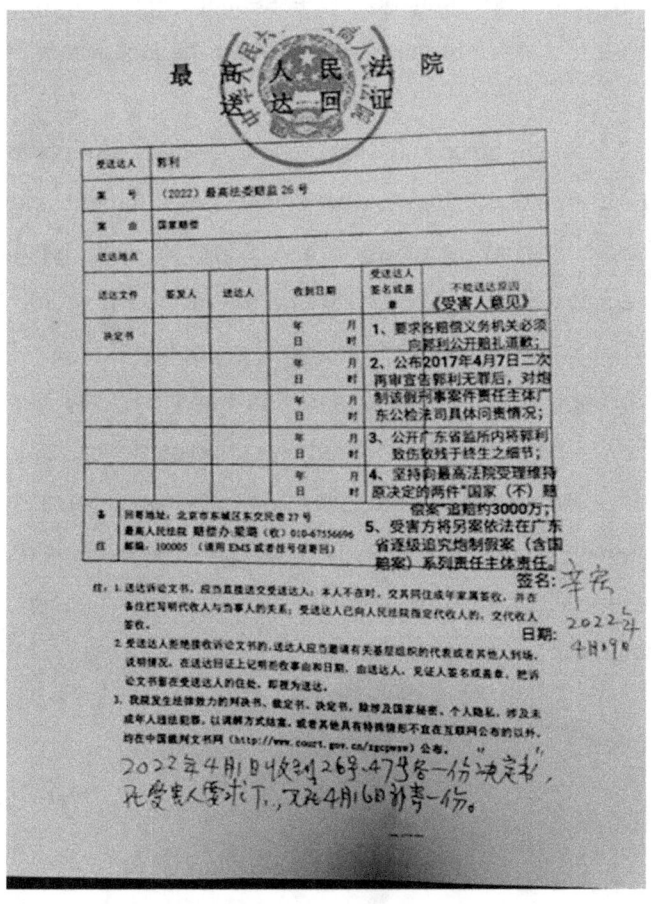

Receipt of Guo, Li's requirement on his

State Compensation case to the Supreme Court of China

have not been able to move in to stay and live for more than five years and it looks like to be continued too! My only limited living space and life in Beijing of China have been squeezed and threatened by such a tragic land. So at the beginning of wider outbreak of the Covid-19 pandemic in 2020, I began to flee all over the country, and finally had to went aboard as exiling, so as to continue my essential medical treatment, surgeries, a life of freedom and fight for the just in rest of my life!

Today, the poisoning effect of tainted-baby formula to me and my family continues. The unjust imprisonment and my lifelong disability after the milk scandals will have an irreversible impact on the child and me in the whole life. The child is still frail and sickly, refusing to accept her father, who is still fighting for her interest and has been severely harmed twice. There are also hundreds of thousands of "Chinese Kidney-stone-Babies" and their parents who have been diagnosed all over the country, and the adverse reactions in their health due to the sequelae caused by melamine still continue and are irreversible.

# Chapter 7.

# Traveled to HK, denied by legal aid, wrote open letters to Mengniu / Yashily

Screenshot of Guizhou Satellite TV on Yashily's formula scandal

At the same time as my state compensation case was being processed, we also filed a claim for the civil compensation against COFCO Mengniu Yashily International in Hong Kong. Since Yashily took the initiative to negotiate compensation with my family in July 2009, and I have been acquitted by Guangdong Provincial High Court after eight years. The child's lifelong harm caused by the Scient melamine-poisoned baby formula, as well as their secondary harm to me and my family caused by the framing case of "collusion between officials and businessman" between Mengniu Yashily and the CCP's local and high-level officials, Yashily and its corporate acquirer COFCO Mengniu Dairy, should be held accountable and compensated.

A year after I was framed up, arrested and imprisoned trans-provincially in Beijing, Zhejiang, and Guangdong provinces, Yashily International was finally listed publicly in

Hong Kong through a series of illegal capital operations, shortly after it was acquired by Mengniu Dairy, a super-large dairy company controlled by the state-owned COFCO Group under the State Council of China. Therefore, it is only natural and imperative that we choose to go to Hong Kong to claim legal civic corporate compensation.

Regarding the legal and procedural issues related to Yashily's fraudulent listing and frame-up the consumer and Hong Kong litigation, after learning from the Hong Kong courts and the government's legal aid department, we found that due to differences in social systems and the way of thinking, there are big differences of the laws, institutional settings, and case filing procedures between mainland China and Hong Kong. If you rely solely on your own strength, not only will it be impossible to achieve it at the technical level such as financial resources and professional legal support, but it will also be extremely difficult to pursue Yashily International and China Mengniu Group through legal procedures in Hong Kong. Therefore, after research, it was decided to apply for legal aid from the Hong Kong Legal Aid Department.

During this period, we visited Yashily International's headquarters in COFCO in Hong Kong to continue to pursue corporate accountability against Yashily and its subsidiary Scient Conpany. After several visits, Yashily's shareholders, China Mengniu Co., Ltd. and COFCO, turned us away from COFCO Mansion. After that, we were interviewed by the

Screenshot from interviewing with Guo, Li,

after Mengniu Dairy acquired Yashily in Hong Kong

medias, including HK Cable TV, Radio Television Hong Kong, Hong Kong Chinese University, and Apple Daily. One of the programs was titled with "No Arrows Turning Back from the Bow". The Department of Journalism of the Chinese University of Hong Kong conducted an interview on my rights defending campaign called "University Line". After the above-mentioned news and special programs were broadcast, they immediately aroused strong public attention, opinion and repercussions in the two sides of the Taiwan Strait and the Three Places (Hong Kong, Macao and Taiwan). Because of the food safety problems and consumer concerns caused by melamine-poisoned formula in China, the influence becomes worldwide. Even the world-renowned Chinese COFCO Group, Cadbury of United Kingdom, Kraft of United States and Canada's former pet food giants have not been immune to this.

In China, when I traveled back and forth to Guangzhou, Chaozhou, Jieyang and other places to read the case file, submit the state compensation package and ask for reconsideration, Vision column group from Tencent, one of the largest internet company in China, conducted a follow-up interview with me, their program produced afterward caused follow-up repercussions on the internet. Nearly 10 years after the outbreak of the melamine-formula scandal, the influence of Guo, Li's deeds of fighting alone and defending my rights has not diminished even in the slightest. On the contrary, the food safety issues in China and even involving SARs of Hong Kong and Macao will become very noisy, concerned and strengthened for a considerable period of time in the future because of the repeated reminders of stories and media.

When I went to Hong Kong to defend my rights, I also kept the cost of the travel to the lowest possible level. The trip from Beijing to Hong Kong is nearly 3,000 kilometers' distance, so we all use the most economical class (green) trains to travel.

Once, I took the Z97 train (from Beijing Railway West Station to Kowloon Station) to Hong Kong via Guangzhou. At about 23:00 o'clock of the night, after the train announcement had told the passengers in the carriage an hour earlier to turn off the lights and rest in sleepers, next to the No. 13 hard-sleeper I booked, two Hong Kong passengers in their 60s with a Beijing accent in berths 15 and 16 were still making loud noises and chatting. We couldn't sleep because of the noise. So I asked them to stop chatting, not to make noise, and not to disturb the rest of other passengers. When two passengers heard this, they complained that I was nosy and had nothing to do with my reminder, so they ignored it and continued chatting. In desperation, I walked to the conductor's room at the junction of the carriages and explained the situation to the conductor. The conductor then followed me to the berths of two passengers and advised them to go to the berths to sleep. As a result, before I could say a word, they slapped me in the face in front of the conductor. At this moment, I immediately proposed to the conductor to report the incident to the police on the train in accordance with the law and train management regulations, but the conductor ignored it.

After a while, when the conductor and the police came to deal with it, they told me that the other part accused me of beating them. It can also be corroborated by the written testimony of multiple other passengers in the same carriage. Isn't this simply a lie? In particular, the conductor, and the male passenger who was chatting and obviously beat me in front of her, not only did she not explain the true circumstances of what happened, but instead acted as a "protective umbrella" for the passenger who beat me, and also gave the above-mentioned false testimony of other passengers. It is estimated that the conductor saw that my attitude towards investigation was particularly firm, and her colleagues did not want to deal with it thoroughly in accordance with the law, so they took the approach of persuading more than a dozen other passengers to give false testimony, and put pressure on me in disguise to force me to calm down according to their plan and will. But my character, even though it's already the middle of the night, still doesn't want to calm things down and let them succeed. There was a passenger in the carriage who couldn't stand it anymore and took the initiative to stand up and testify that it was the male passenger who beat me. The two passengers not only made a loud noise after 23:00 o'clock, disturbed others, did not stop after being dissuaded, but also beat the passenger Guo, Li in anger. Early next morning, I told the conductor and the police that surveillance video cameras were installed at both ends of the train carriages, and for the sake of fairness, I implored them to obtain the surveillance video records of the carriages after the train arrived at the Hong Kong (Kowloon)

The passenger who made noise and disturbed others in the train

then fled away after

Railway Station, so as to use this as a basis for handling the disputed issue impartially in accordance with the law.

When the train arrived at Hong Kong Kowloon Station, just as everyone was packing up their luggage, preparing to get off the train, in an emergency situation where no one was paying attention to my claims, I took the opportunity to stop the two

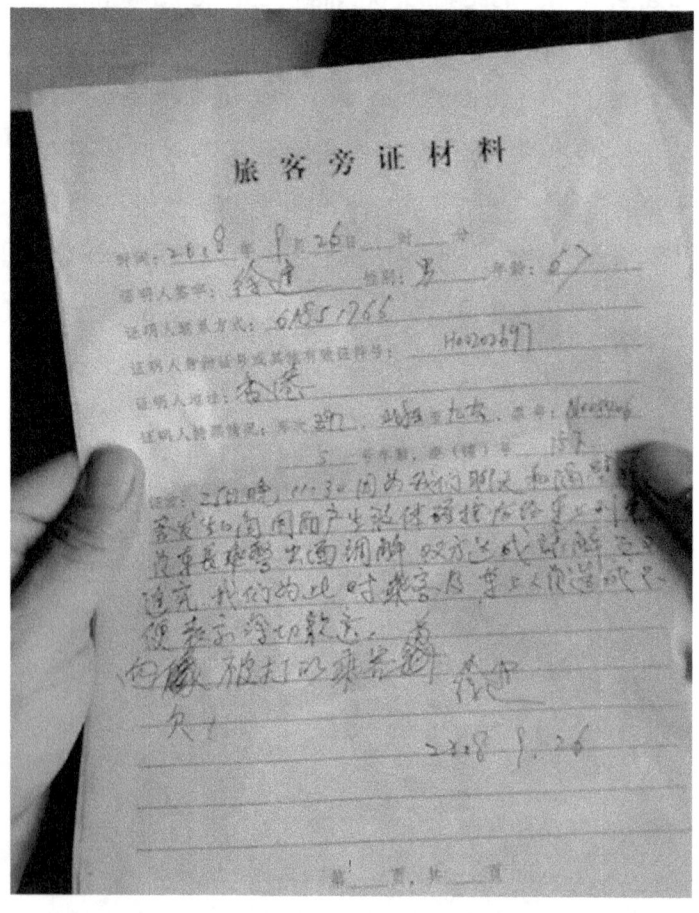

The written apology for the issue in the train by the "fled-away"

passenger

passengers who beat me, and called the Z97 conductor and the police again, asked them to go to the Kowloon Station Police Office to conduct a thorough investigation of the beating incident that occurred in the train last night. At this time, I only saw the male passenger who hit me panicked, and his female companion was also at a loss. For this reason they begged me vigorously to let them go. At this time, the police and the conductor also felt bad, and asked the two to write a letter of apology with a statement of the situation and sign it to me. At this time, the train happened to enter the platform and open the door, and the two passengers and the rest of others in the same carriage who had helped them to commit perjury fled

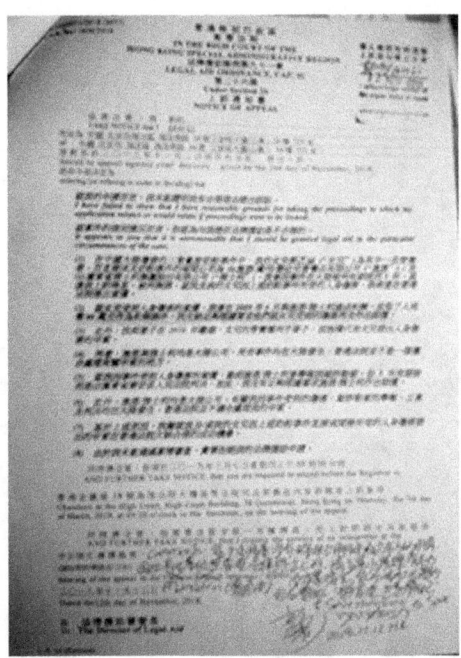

Records from the High Court of Hong Kong about Guo's case

quickly and disappeared without a trace. Similar things have happened several times in the course of my years of defending the rights, even happened nowadays when I am writing this book in North America. The disappointment and sadness in it are unknown to no one, and perhaps even more incomprehensible. But I think it's just a testament to the tenacity and perseverance of my character, that is, if I think it is right and do the right thing, I will stick to it and do it thoroughly.

In order to apply for legal aid from the Legal Aid Department of Hong Kong, we have prepared a lot of materials as required, including proof of our funds and a plan to sue Yashily International, which we have submitted. Soon after review, the Legal Aid Department of Hong Kong gave us a reply that they did not approve our application for assistance.

Guo and his mother, in front of High Court in Hong Kong

The general reason is that we are not qualified to sue Yashily International and China Mengniu Dairy Group in the Hong Kong SAR, and they believe that I am a citizen of the mainland China, and these issues should be civil and criminal cases under the jurisdiction of the Chinese mainland. The Hong Kong courts only trial cases and disputes involving Hong Kong citizens and those arising in the Hong Kong jurisdictions. However, we believe that as its victim consumers, we have the right to pursue 'cross-regional' investigation and litigation of the poisoned baby formula company Yashily and its holding China Mengniu Dairy Company for suspected cross-regional related infringement compensation and cross-border food business crimes. Accordingly, after the Legal Aid Department dismissed our application, we filed an appeal with the High Court of Hong Kong. After a simple investigation process, The High Court also rejected our legal claim on the same grounds as the Legal Aid Department.

The successive setbacks of Hong Kong Government's Legal Aid Department and the High Court, as well as misunderstandings in the media's coverage of the legal matter make the public think that we have filed a lawsuit against Yashily International and its shareholder China Mengniu Dairy in the Hong Kong law court. In fact, the High Court of Hong Kong directly denied the feasibility of me, as a victim, to sue the 'Evil Forces' enterprise for infringement and compensation.

There are many obstacles that make it impossible to file a

case in Hong Kong. The High Court upheld the Legal Aid Department's view that I was not qualified to pursue further proceedings against Yashily Dairy in Hong Kong. My understanding of this issue is that with the so called "One-Country-Two-Systems" principle only exists in its name, the rule of law is no longer there, and Hong Kong has become a dead PORT (meaning a dead HK in mandarin). There are differences between the mainland and Hong Kong in terms of humanities, culture, and law enforcement. In addition, they believe that I have divorced my ex-wife and lost custody of the child, which means that I have lost the right to claim compensation under the HK law. But they ignored the fact that I was forced to divorce in prison because I was wrongly convicted by mainland Chinese courts, and the actual custody of the child was not in the hands of my ex-wife. In this particular environment, there are specific circumstances that many legal practitioners have never encountered and cannot understand. When both the Legal Aid Department of Hong Kong and the High Court have determined that, I, as a victim of infringement, cannot sue the dairy companies as we called them "Evil Forces"(雅士利 or 雅势力 in Mandarin) in Hong Kong, our accusation seems to be in vain.

In fact, defending rights in Hong Kong is similar to defending rights in the mainland China, which means that it will be difficult and challenging. After I was released from prison, I basically planned and completed it by myself, with my mother XIN's limited assistance. The reality is that there are very few people who really dare or can help me and my family in China. In the process of defending my rights, the friends who can help me are basically two or three people who help typing and copying, sorting out our verbal materials, and providing professional advice or assistance in financial accounting. One of the most helpful to me was an accountant YZ and an engineer SLZ who helped calculate and record the content of the case claim and related writing data.

Reports, interviews and commentaries from the free world medias outside mainland China on my struggle and legal right defending, such as the Chinese University of Hong Kong, Apple Daily, Australian Financial Review, Radio Free Asia, and Voice of America, have attracted the attention of the Chinese police and even national security authority (intelligent agency) .

One of my accountant friend said that since the medias reported on our trip to Hong Kong to defend my legal rights, the Beijing police had been to her parents' homes several times. Because my friend does not live there, there are always some "unknown" people claiming to be police officers who come to harass her parents, and the elderlies in the family are very nervous and worried. In particular, on February 17th 2019, the friend called me and told me that a police officer surnamed Ma from Beijing Municipal Public Security Bureau (police station), who claimed to be the director of a department, had repeatedly asked her to meet at a Costa café opposite the Workers' Gymnasium in Dongcheng District of Beijing and she just planned to go there as the police asked. When I got the call, I quickly rushed to the café to find out what was going on, found a corner seat inside and sit down, began to make a video recording of the meeting in real time. I felt that the atmosphere in the café was abnormal, there were a lot of customers present that day, about 20 people, and it didn't look like they were 'together', but their facial expressions were all serious and strange.

After my friend entered the café, she was questioned in detail by a police team led by an officer chief called Ma from the Beijing City Police. Ma specially asked: What is the matter with Guo, Li? What is Guo, Li doing? How is Guo's child doing? My friend replied: You should ask Guo, Li himself these questions, this is his personal privacy. Ma asked her again: Why did you help Guo, Li? The Friend said that because Guo, Li was disabled in jail, there was no way to complete his rights defending alone, and his mother XIN Hong also suffered a fracture after a fall and had to go out in a wheelchair, so she needed to be taken care of by someone else; Both of them are currently disabled, and as their friends, She will naturally sympathize with them, and can only help a little bit.

Ma then asked: What did Guo, Li do when he went to Hong Kong? The friend replied: It was Guo, Li who pursued Yashily's rights defending in accordance with the law. Because Yashily is listed publicly in Hong Kong, and its headquarters is also located there, he went to Hong Kong to do these things. Ma asked my friend's workplace and home address again. At this point, my friend sensed a threat from them. In the meantime, my friend told Ma and the police team in words, asking them not to harass their families in Beijing in the future, and to go directly to her if there is something to do. Towards the end of the conversation, Chief Ma specially added: You have to use your brain, don't break the law and violate the act. Guo, Li is just a friend of yours, you don't have to put your own at risk, don't seek ZhanBaoEr or trouble for yourself ("ZhanBaoER" means getting into a big trouble in Beijing dialect), you have your elderly at home....

About half an hour later, Chief Ma finished talking with my friend and was getting up to leave, and just as he walked out of the café door, someone hurried out the door to report to him that he saw someone taking pictures of them in the café. Suddenly, Ma and the other three police returned to the café again, and at a glance, they saw me sitting in the corner and taking pictures of them. He walked up to me, sat down and

A scene photo in the café,

lots of plain cloth Beijing police sitting and ambushed around there

asked, "Are you Guo, Li? Why are you here?" I replied: why can't I be here? He said, "Can we talk?" I said, "Yes." Then his assistants found the cane I carried, and immediately reached over and tried to take it away. I immediately yelled at him, said: "Don't touch it, you can't take it, it's my walking stick to help me walk."

Then one of the police team came to me and said, "You can't attack us with a cane." I replied that I had a fracture, and a spine injury. Travel must rely on the cane to help; why should I attack you with my walk cane? After taking the seats one after another, Ma asked me: "What are you doing?" I discovered and realized that Ma didn't really know much about my case. Then I gave him a general introduction to the melamine-poison-formula incident and the circumstances of my current case. After listening to my explanation, I thought they were going to take me away to the police station at that time. As a result, Ma said, "Okay, let's finish the talk for today, all withdraw!" As soon as he gave the order, more than 20 people in the café got up almost simultaneously and quickly evacuated from the Costa café.

It turned out that my feeling was indeed correct. These more than 20 people were all from them. They were all plainclothes polices from the four departments of Dongcheng, Xicheng, Chaoyang District and Beijing City Police Headquarters. Because my friend's household registration is in Xicheng District, her workplace is in Chaoyang District, and her family lives in Dongcheng District, so Police Chief Ma said during the interview: It's really troublesome, and we need to cooperate with the police from three districts before we can meet you here.

When I mention these episodes in the process of rights defending and fight, I don't just want to express how difficult

Photo of Zou, Pengliang, police chief in Chao`an, Guangdong

and challenging the process of rights defending is; In fact, I also want to explain that in my own story of overturning the case and defending my legal rights, I have also received the attention or help of some friends and departments. I still want to express that the impact of melamine-poison-formula on our country, and even the world's food safety and consumers' environment is huge! For this reason, I think it is very meaningful to persevere, to improve the food and safety environment in both China and the world, to the progress of the country's judiciary, and to our future improvement or reforms.

After my proposed lawsuit in Hong Kong's against Yashily International, China Mengniu Group, its former Chairman

Photo of Zhong, Ming, former police chief

in Chaozhou, Guangdong, later was jailed

Zhang Litian and others was not supported and refused to be accepted by the Legal Aid Department and the High Court of Hong Kong, I still did not give up. Since 2018, I have issued "An Open Letter To Yashily International" and will continue to pursue denunciations in China, Hong Kong SAR and North America on it.

In order to submit the open letter, we also came to Yashily International's headquarters in Guangzhou several times at the same time. Since one of the culprits in concocting this unjust, false and wrongful case was Zhang Litian, former Chair of Yashily International Group in Guangdong and Hong Kong, who is also a delegate in Chinese National People's Congress. To investigate his criminal liability, it is necessary to report to the relevant National People's Congress Standing Committee.

After receiving a reply from the Guangdong Provincial People's Congress that we could report to the National People's Congress in Beijing to hold Zhang Litian and his legal counsel Wu Xiaonan etc. accountable, we also went to the Criminal Investigation Section of Guangdong Provincial Public Security Department to report the criminal clues and investigation issues of the false accusations and frame-ups by Zhang, Wu and others. Also we reported the case to the Chaozhou Public Security Bureau (police) where the incident occurred.

Guo Jinqing, formal Prosecutor at Chaozhou , Guangdong, who took Guo Li`s case and wrongful prosecuted in 2009

However, in the process of accusation, for some reason, once the responsibility of Yashily International Group for violating the law was involved, various departments were still

## 致 雅士利（國際）乳業公開信

A Letter from the Victims to Yashily Dairy 2018

雅士利&施恩公司：

本人是貴公司 2008 年三聚氰胺毒奶粉事件中受害兒童父親，實際被害人郭利，北京市民。

2009 年 4 月至 7 月間，貴公司（原廣東雅士利集團&施恩 Scient 公司）因制造销售了"美囿施恩牌"三聚氰胺嬰幼兒毒奶粉，向消費者進行虛假宣傳此品牌及其奶源（100%）來自美囿等……。期間，被本人在依法維權過程中發現了真相。由於雅士利惧怕東窗事發，於是精心策划了 2009 年那場"钓鱼式賠償談判"，蓄意無中生有，製造"結石寶寶父親郭利敲詐勒索案"。當年參與報此案的是貴公司總裁張利鈿、律師吳曉楠、北區總監段庚惠等高管數人。當年，在子虛烏有的造假案過程中，貴公司曾诱导本人草擬了一個索賠 300 萬元的賠償協議。該協議也由貴公司承諾將承兑履行。然而該協議經貴司約定在杭州市付款前夕，本人即被貴公司生產所在地的廣東潮州公安機關"跨省抓獲歸案"。

9 年多过去了，本人的無罪申诉也换来了廣東省检方和省高院的法定認可："无论索賠多少，郭利均是在行使索賠权利。厂家不同意其索賠数額，则属于有争议的民事法律关系。郭利

1 / 4

The open letter written to the Yashily Dairy from Guo, Li

protecting and exculpating the criminal responsibility of Zhang Litian and Wu Xiaonan of the "Yashily Forces"（meaning Evil Forces in Mandarin）, and even took the initiative to take responsibility in the form of "civil public power". So far, the false accusations and frame-ups carried out by Zhang and his gang against the victim Guo, Li have not been investigated and reflected in any way; And Zhang's personal whereabouts have become a mystery to this day. I was falsely accused of "extortion" in the case of a number of policemen, prosecutors, judges, prison guards, and the persons in charge of the case-handling authorities, and almost all of them have since been brought to justice.

In addition to submitting my open letters to Yashily International, China Mengniu Group and the Hong Kong High Court, I also submitted materials to the Hong Kong Securities and Futures Commission to expose and report Yashily International's fraudulent going public and defrauding shareholders issues in Hong Kong SAR. But the Securities and Futures Commission of Hong Kong ignored this.

In the past sixteen years, I have always focused on overturning my unjust case and making full compensation(s) and safeguarding my legal rights. However, the whole process is full of thorns and dangers, and is not understood even by my family members. They often feel very tired of these and think that preparing so many materials and sending so many letters is of no use! Many people in the internet (Netizens or "WangYou") also left messages in the places under media reports about me. In addition to most of them expressing their admiration for my spirit of persistence and pursuit, a few critical also questioned my approach. For example, one of them left a message under former Hong Kong Apple Daily report about me: Guo, Li, you are a Mainlander (from Beijing China), and you went to Hong Kong to defend your rights. Is it because Hong Kong will compensate you more money? The ideas of some people are utilitarian and are incompatible with my concept of rights defending and fight.

The energy, financial resources and enthusiasm of ordinary people will be exhausted in this long and difficult journey, but I am always a lonely fighter. My road of rights defending and fight will continue to be pursued and implemented. But I really wish I don't have to go into my 3rd eight years of life for this.

### 【Don't Talk About】 2009-2024

Guo, Li's Compensation Case - The "Sixteen Years of Resistance War" with repeated defeats and battles

"Even if law enforcement agencies such as the Ministry of Public Security and the Justice do not abide by the law, I will also insist on completing the judicial process in accordance with the law."

Just like climbing Mount Everest, the North Slope tests your physical strength even more.

The South Slope is more technical and there is no absolute difficulty and easiness.

The ultimate goal is to conquer it!

There is no turning back when the bow is drawn,

No matter how difficult and hopeless it is, we must

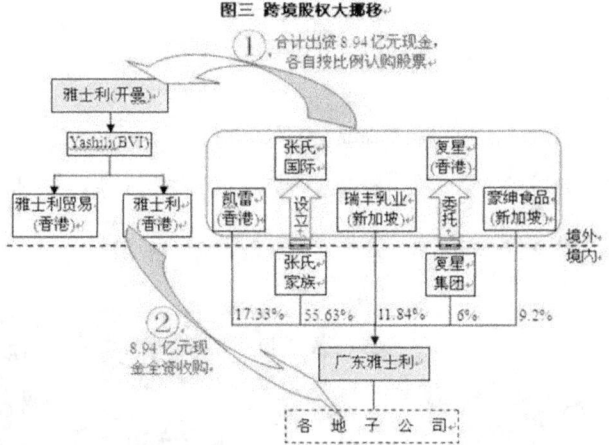

Chart of Yashily's running structure

and going-global development

persevere.

More than a dozen departments and more than 20 judgments

Submitted "In accordance with the Law" again and again,

The "Illusions" were shattered again and again,

What awaits U is "Not Accepted" and "Lack of Factual Basis"

"Does not fall within the Scope of State Compensation", "No Compensation",

"Reject", "Dismissed", "Maintain in accordance with the Law..."

"Legally speaking,

If the judiciary wrongfully accuses a person,

He was ultimately found innocent.

香港蘋果日報
43 分鐘 ·

郭利的女兒，是10年前毒奶粉事件受害者之一。為了討回公道，即使身陷冤獄、妻離女散，他也要走下去。開弓之箭，不回頭。

【結石寶寶堅毅爸爸　五年冤獄　箭不回頭】
http://bit.ly/2lzHTCr ←短片

hk.news.appledaily.com
【動畫】毒奶粉公司在港註冊　結石寶寶爸來港討公道
【維權父親】今年是內地毒奶粉事件10周年，「結石寶寶」爸...

News about Guo, Li on Apple Daily of Hong Kong

They should take the initiative to compensate (the victim part)."

Guangdong High Court declared Guo, Li not guilty to this day.

It's been sixteen years.

They did not apologize for the disability to Guo, Li caused by the prison.

There was no judicial return of private property for illegal seizure of my home.

There is no judicial process for cross-examination in court.

In some cases, the notification of filing a case was almost lost.

Some witnesses and friends were threatened one after another.

Some cases are just revoked and have exceeded the two-year statute of limitations.

Everything is cleared empty!

What cannot be cleared away is the permanent damage to Guo, Li

Regarding the initial explanation of disability in the Chinese jails,

The Chaozhou Intermediate People's Court held that "although we made a wrong judgment, but we didn't instruct the police or prison to beat you to be disabled."

"Whoever hurts and harms you is the one you should sue."

The Guangdong High Court believes that "other legal channels can be used to solve the compensation issues"

At that time you didn't raise the issue of a Statute of Limitations exceeding two years!

In order to "prove" that I am not disabled during the jailing term,

Just say that I can participate in the arranged labor-work normally,

In order to "prove" that I did not plead guilty and my

# 雅士利上市的隐秘

这家乳业公司上市过程中，一直隐现着两个神秘的"独立第三方"

■ 文/苏龙飞 刘基

## Untold Story behind Yashili's Listing

On November 1st, 2010, the first day of its listing in Hong Kong, Yashili closed 13% lower than its IPO price which was set at HKD4.2. Despite its unsatisfactory IPO price and first-day trend, the infant dairy company founded jointly by 6 brothers from a certain Zhang's family in the Chaozhou-Shantou area

One of the reports from media (AFR)

about secrets of Yashily's going public

sentence was not reduced,

They just provide a certificate saying that I basically don't participate in the labor-reform.

You testify against each other.

"They all said it was an injury from outside world before coming here."

Falsifying various medical examination documents inside the prison system.

It cannot be justified at all.

Questions:

In the same country, in the same province,

Do the same type of state compensation cases,

However, different legal judgment results can occur.

It is ridiculous and rare in the world.

Why were the victim's milk powder and valuables involving the police infringement of property rights cases,

can partially be awarded or compensated "Arbitrarily"?

One judgment is valid and the other is invalid;

A case within a case can lead to different judgments.

The result is opposite. Where is the reason? What is the basis?

I requested the prison to compensate for the damage caused to my body,

Cases of human rights violations also involving permanent mental disability,

After local court filed the case, the case was "Hastily-Wind-Up" and then Revoked?

But they failed to clarify each case, make a determination and give DUE compensation?

Even the most basic issue like:

Making a PUBLIC apology to the victim part in accordance with the law

Have they all been exempted from their "violation of the law"?

What's the intention?

Using "a hurried withdrawal" of cases that have been filed according to law for another purpose!

And trying to hide the truth.

What kind of plot could be behind it?

"Don't hire a counsel, just defend yourself",

The eight-year "war of resistance" for my state compensation,

Overcome unimaginable difficulties and challenges,

Use walking cane, push wheelchairs,

With my elderly and sick mother,

Carrying "heavy" case materials,

A variety of medications for basic diseases,

Take the slowest green train,

Traveled to & from Beijing, Guangdong and Hong Kong dozens of times,

From winter to summer,

In the cycle of expectation and disappointment...

Take every step steadily for the rest of my life,

The case was submitted to the Supreme Procuratorate

The issue of "state (non-)compensation" was raised....

Prosecutorial supervision, filing of cases, accountability and protests....

Justice...?

The legal distance between "what is said and what is (not) done"

Is it all drifting away? ?

Let's WAIT and SEE!

Guo is sewing one screenshot of his interviews to the front side of a

hoody

Chapter 8.

# Guo's adventures during exiles for his overseas rights defending

In early February 2020, at the invitation of Mr. Rr. Z from the University of Alberta Business School, I traveled from Washington, USA to British Columbia, Canada, and then took a long distance train for two nights to arrive in Edmonton, the capital of Alberta, and began traveling and planning cooperation on interviews and case studies on the topic "Melamine-Milk Scandal and Novel Coronavirus".

At that time, the coronavirus epidemic was raging in China, but its impact overseas was relatively small or negligible at first. I had planned to stay for two weeks in Canada. After arriving at the University of Alberta, Mr. Rr. Z and the professor who was nominated for the Nobel Prize in Economics were interested in seeing me, even though they were nearing their senior age. I had made an appointment with them to have a meeting, but when they heard that I was crossing the border from Hong Kong of China, I was told that the meeting was cancelled for fear of the possible spread of the Covid-19 virus. Over the next two weeks, a total of five episodes were made on the topic of "melamine-milk and novel coronavirus". Just as I was about to end my visit to the University of Alberta with Mr. Rr. Z. We suddenly heard that the border between United States and Canada was completely closed. Because the epidemic was raging and the border was completely closed, I could not leave, so I had to stay in Alberta, wait and see what would happen, maintaining an unpredictable and extremely simple quarantine life. It is also impossible to realize the plan and arrangement of my own continued travel. I heard that the senior professor who was unable to meet due to the spread of the epidemic was hospitalized due to catching the novel

Guo, Li, in front of a bus stop in Canada

coronavirus, his life was also in critical condition, and he was not spared the catastrophe.

Being forced to remain in Alberta, my budget for food, clothing, housing and transportation became a top priority. The border between the United States and Canada was closed out of my expectation, and I didn't know when it would be lifted. I could only go to a property agency to look for affordable housing to rent.

By coincidence, my first landlord called Lao Zhang, was an investment immigrant from Tianjin of China lived here more than ten years ago. Zhang's wife Xiao Du, is a Beijing-born Hutonger girl who studied at the University of Waterloo a few years ago. They have two children in Canada. Zhang's rental house is a very old two-story single-family house with five bedrooms. Soon after buying it, they decorated it and turned it into an Airbnb lodging for their self-employment and livelihood. On the floor of basement of the house, a Canadian young man who worked in IT business once rented a bedroom. The young man was over 1.9 meters tall and in a very good health. According to his own introduction, his financial situation is very good, with a monthly salary of tens of thousands of Canadian dollars. There was also a local Canadian girl living in another room of the basement. She had a pet dog named Nelly. I live in the master bedroom on the first floor of Zhang's house.

What's interesting is that the local girl often goes out at night, saying that her company has night shifts of bookkeeping to do. After getting to know each other in a short period of time, she would often ask us to help taking care of or feeding her pet dog Nelly. Over time, we became like a family!

The pet dog Nelly

After a while, I also saw this local girl riding in and out of the big young guy's car and taking the dog for a walk, and they behaved very pleasantly. It turned out that... they were just in love. One day, I heard something strange and moving downstairs. After a while, I decided to go down and take a look. Oh..., it turned out to be the young man sitting at the side door crying. I curiously asked him what was wrong. He said he had nothing left, including his wallet, keys and his car parking outside. In other words, from the day before to when he woke up minutes ago, he had been unconsciously sleeping in his bedroom downstairs for a whole day. Afterwards, his father who came over told us that he was sent to a nearby hospital for seven days treatment. When the young man left to go to the hospital, I went downstairs again and found that the padlock outside his room was not locked, so I subconsciously locked the padlock for him. In the meantime, the local girl came back in the young man's car, and I saw her and another man coming over to carry something out from the house.

The landlord Zhang, was still there at this time. I went to him and told him that someone was moving something suspiciously out from his house and asked him to call the police if needed. Unexpectedly, Zhang said to us: Don't do it and mind your own business! Two days later, the young man's father came over from out of town, and we helped him open the bedroom of his son. At this time, his father especially thanked me, saying that his son had been drugged into a coma and had been robbed. Fortunately, I locked the door to his bedroom earlier. Otherwise, if the local girl came back and removed his son's work computer and other hardware items from his bedroom, it would be really troublesome and the economic loss would be even greater. At this time, our landlord Zhang went downstairs to take a look, only to find that the local girl and the above-mentioned outsider had looted the furniture he used to open the lodging, as well as all items such as quilts and bedcovers for guest uses. Zhang regretted it so much for not reporting to the police the earliest he could. After calling the 911, the police came and said that they had noticed this criminal gang for a long time and asked us to take more precautions and call the police in time without further delay. Later, I heard from the police that the young man's car was found hundreds of kilometers away of Edmonton. In other words, after committing the crime, the local girl and the gang members abandoned the vehicle in the woods in a remote suburb.

In addition to being timid and afraid of getting into trouble, Zhang also has a "profit-only" characteristic. In order to make the rent higher, he basically chooses short-term rental (usually within 30 days) customers. After this rental period, he will not renew the lease.

Guo and the pet dog Nelly

However the Ministry of Housing and Social Development has

strict legal protection measures and policies for tenancy issues. In other words, the landlord cannot evict or move any legal tenant without a RTB judgment. Because we are both Asians, and I got to know the landlord Zhang and his wife Du. One day, he told me that his home had encountered tenants who refused to move out, and one of the methods he used was to apply the poison gas into the heating system. At that time, I had been renting his house for more than a month. I originally thought he was threatening me and driving me away. But later I found out that what Zhang did was real and true, it had really happened. In fact, I helped him a lot later. Once Zhang said that he wanted to invest in real estate in the Banff scenic spot, and he specifically asked me for suggestion and opinion.

I was consulted for this purpose. I said that depending on the spread of the epidemic and the global economic situation, it is recommended not to invest in real estate, and to wait for three years before making a decision.... This time, he should have listened to my advice and avoided the risks and losses caused by the following three years of the Covid-19 crisis and recession of local tourism business.

In order to facilitate academic exchanges and reduce rent expense, I left Zhang's lodging soon after. I rent another room closer to the University of Alberta. Coincidentally, the landlord is also Chinese, and called Xiao Tan, an international student from Jiujiang City of Jiangxi Province in China, who graduated from the University of Alberta. Tan's family is well-off, and his mother bought him a property in Canada at earlier time. Living in his own house, Tan rent out the spare rooms to earn income. Among the tenants, one is a Chinese international student, nicknamed Master Rabbit, who lives in the most expensive bedroom of the house, paid monthly rent of about 1,500 Canadian dollars. During the period of the epidemic, students were not allowed to go to school. I found that Xiao Tan and Master Rabbit were actually very difficult in learning and study of the courses, they even could not communicate fluently in English at all. Through my observation, what I find is that they are playing video games during the school hours, not to mention learning or study at home.

After communicating with Tan, I found out that their grades were indeed very bad; although the University of Alberta is ranked among the top 100 universities in the world, many of these international students passed the exam by using "gunman". One day Master Rabbit had a little conflict with me, because he deliberately made noise in the house. I kindly reminded him but there were still no effect and convergence. The landlord Tan asked me to leave immediately with a deposit

Guo with the pet cat Kikino

return, but there was no legal reason for him to let me move out like this. The reason he has is the Master Rabbit told him that he did not agree with me to continue to live here. So, I theorized with landlord Tan in accordance with the rental regulations, saying: Tan, you ARE the landlord, not someone who gives you more rent can have the final say, if you force me out of this rental issue in unreasonable way, then you can't stay in Canada as well. Tan saw that my reason was reasonable and modest, and my attitude was tough, so he didn't mention the issue again. Master Rabbit didn't dare to mention the issue that I had to move out.

I still live on the first floor of a modified mezzanine garage, but I often hear noisy footsteps upstairs and downstairs and the sounds of outsiders, and sometimes it feels like there are still a lot of people, as if they are partying or something. Because I couldn't resist my curiosity, one day I finally walked down the basement floor, and saw that the largest living room downstairs was arranged like a conference hall, with traces of meetings and logos on the wall. A check on the Internet by me turned out to be a branch venue of the Communist Youth League under the United Front Work Department of China, which was holding a meeting overseas.

After renting Tan's house for half a year, the visit to the University of Alberta and the epidemic lockdown came to an end. And eight months ago I planned to visit Xiao Gao, another Zhejiang friend in Gatineau of Quebec, but due to the unforeseeable obstacles he encountered, I was forced to take a train to Ottawa, the capital of Canada, as the next temporarily stop of my 'blind' type of travel during the epidemic.

Four months after arriving in the capital, Ottawa, the fourth landlord I met was still Chinese named Lao Zhou. He immigrated to Canada more than 20 years ago from China, after joining a state-owned machinery & equipment trading company in Beijing. Because Zhou had worked in foreign trade, he and his family finally chose to settle in Ottawa after visiting and investigating several developed countries. According to Zhou, he has four mid-range properties in Ottawa region of Canada; I rented a renovated living room in one of his single houses. The house is divided into three floors, with 3 bedrooms for rent on the basement floor, 2 rooms for rent on the ground floor, and the original 4 rooms on the second floor. I stayed in the room with lowest rent which is on the ground floor where the living room was divided and partitioned.

After meeting compatriots in a foreign country, our rental agreement was originally agreed and signed, it will take effect on the first day of the next month. But Zhou was very

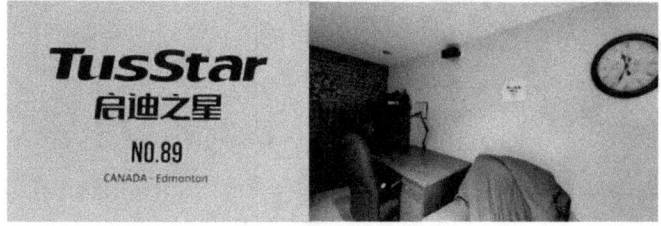

The underground assembly place

Place No. 89 for TSCE

enthusiastic, even invited me to move in a week in advance: "You can move in a few days in advance, Guo". I don't really like to take advantage of landlord for this, especially if there is a contract, so I politely declined. But when I packed my bags at the end of the month and was ready to move into my new house on the first day of the coming month, when our moving van drove to the house, I saw something unusual happening. There are heavy smoke and traces of burning inside and outside the house, muddy water flows on the ground inside and

Photo of the room after fire

outside the courtyard, garbage and furniture are piled up outside the main door, and several workers were busy. When Zhou saw me coming, he looked crying, stammering in Hunan-accented Mandarin that the property had accidentally caught fire the day before we came, and that the room that caught fire happened to be the reading room directly opposite the room I rented.

Later, Zhou said that if I had moved in early a few days ago, the fire would not have happened. Ironically, Xiao Liu, the driver who helped me moving, said that before he picked me up, in his car he was playing tape with an old pop song titled as "A Fire in Winter" sung by a Chinese-American singer Fei Xiang. And this fire in winter was really caught.

The cause of the fire turned out to be the day before, a white lady tenant living in the reading room on the first floor lit a candle for her party, and accidentally fell asleep before distinguishing the candle. Later the candle lighted the clothes in her bedroom and everything was on fire.

At the beginning of the fire, the other three tenants who rented on the second floor, a Chinese student, a Vietnam student and an Egyptian pharmacy delivery driver, although they all heard the smoke detector alarm in the living room and smelled a strange odor, but they just took turns downstairs to briefly look around, feeling and thinking that it was just a smoke detector malfunction that caused the alarm similar to what have occurred before, without any big problem, so they didn't care about going upstairs to their rooms again to rest; About fifteen minutes later, as the fire in the downstairs had gotten out of control and was getting bigger and bigger, they all fled outside when they saw the  smoke billowing and the flames were rising to the sky. After the

911 was called, the firefighters rushed to split the door and rescued the lady tenant in the burning room, which was regarded as saving life. The tenants upstairs also expressed their panic. The Chinese student later told me that he was about to jump from the second floor to escape! However, he felt that the floor was a bit high, and he would definitely be injured seriously or fractured if he jumped. Later, he was able to escape by breaking into the door with the help of Sami, the

Guo Li, in front of the buildings of Parliament of Canada

Egyptian driver, running from the second-floor stairs to the front yard in smoke.

Lao Zhou bought insurance for the house. After the fire, we asked him if he had reported to the insurance company. However Zhou repeatedly emphasized that we should not make a noise, he did not want to apply for insurance aid. He didn't want the property fire to be known, with the fear of affecting the market price of the house and subsequent side effect issues. He also said that if he applied for insurance, the

subsequent insurance premiums would increase after, which he felt was not cost-effective. Because of the fire in the house, Zhou successively adopted some technical means, such as: evicting most of his tenants in the house "according to law". The room caught fire was a reading room, which is not allowed to be used for rental according to Canada's residential tenancy laws and relevant

Guo, behind an iron door
in jail

requirements for the rental units. After that, Zhou also adopted some illegal methods commonly used by some Chinese Canadians, such as bribery, hiding the fire of the property and the illegal continued rental after fire, and concealed the past in front of the local city government and its housing leasing department. Zhou had no choice but to put the house for sale many times by various real estate agents or companies, probably because of the fire, even if the price listed was reduced, it seemed difficult to sell it at the price according to his own wishes.

Renting a shelter in Canada, some Chinese Canadians and landlords I met all chose a favorable immigration country to settle in after accumulating the capital in their early stage. Although they are all due to the fact that western countries are far more liberal and democratic, and protect the rights of private property, the various words, deeds, customs and/or behaviors they originally had from their original countries are somewhat incompatible with the current ones. Actually they are also consciously or unintentionally destroying environment and atmosphere where they stay. Of course, they are still very concerned about China's domestic affairs and social environment. For instance, Zhou often inquired and discussed many things with me about China. However, some of the problems and spiritual issues that they have cultivated in China for many years have also been brought to the western world.

Guo, with his doctor

in hospital

A year later, in order to further facilitate medical treatment and surgery, I traveled to Vancouver of British Columbia on the west coast of Canada. Unexpectedly and accidentally, I met a former dairy investor from the China, who is said to have dealt with Niu Gensheng, the founder of China Mengniu Dairy Group in China. He asked me to broadcast a live talk program, at the front gate of a mansion where Niu Gensheng bought in Vancouver, I politely declined. China Mengniu Dairy Group is one of the world's largest dairy enterprises and belongs to COFCO under the State Council of China. The company's founder, Niu Gensheng, is believed to be currently living permanently in Vancouver or has become a Canadian Citizen, and often sponsors various activities in politics and has investments in private funds.

I am very disgusted and resistant to this kind of "two-faced" practice of killing or harming Chinese consumers only for taking their money (谋财害命 in mandarin) and currying favor with the international society and the community of the country where they live! What they earn at home country is

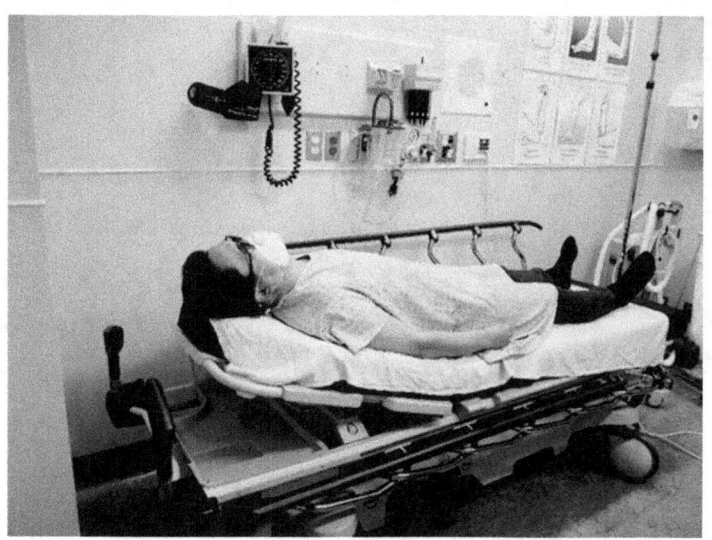

black-hearted money, and those immigrants who transfer assets abroad are just "fishing for their fame and compliments" only, and people who know the real fact really can't approve of it. Make an appointment to find the settlement issue with the Niu? It is nothing more than the issue that once I claimed compensation of 40 million US dollars from Mengniu (Yashily International) Dairy Group. As the founders of China's Mengniu Dairy Group, they may have inquired about my ideas and a book writing or publishing trends. After several years of traveling and adventure abroad, I have neither snobbed to change my nationality, nor enjoyed the free medical treatment of western countries that political immigrants can get; In fact,

these are inseparable from my own personality and principles. In the face of temptation or challenge, the vast majority of people will take the initiative or be forced to choose compromise and opportunism, which is the gap and embodiment of human nature, and the root cause of my firm, independent fight and defending, the last but not the least, I will never give up.

郭利：希望"结石宝宝"悲剧不再重演 | 不惑 2024

Hope my tragedy will not happen again!

Report from the NF Weekend

# A By-Stander's Note

## Humanity: Doing Good----A Winter Trip in 2023

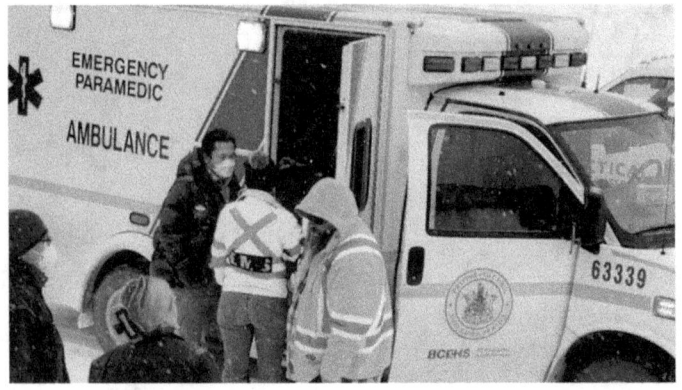

The world-famous Canada Sightseeing Train is something that people here have always longed for. Four of us accidentally formed a group and went on a sightseeing winter trip. Among the four, there is the enthusiastic and cheerful Sister Dong, the Mentor Guo who is proficient in English, the honest and serious Y. Zhang, and I who have never been alone.

On February 24th 2023, we arrived at 14:00 o'clock at Vancouver Pacific Center Station. Although we were randomly grouped, we are all punctual and trustworthy persons. Most of the people waiting in the railway station hall are senior citizens. Maybe because the 19-hour long train ride is too long, some passengers are timid about it, but this is the beginning of our slow life.

I saw a few Asian faces in the passengers in the boarding area. They must be Canadians, a family of six, parents and four children. Because they are specially dressed, they attract our attention even more. The father was dressed in white sportswear, and the mother was wearing a bright red coat. She was holding a one-year-old child in her arms. What I didn't understand was that there were three children accompanying her. And the parents are very conscious about wearing medical masks, especially the father who wears the "very scary" N95 one.

At this time, I had some doubts on him, but I still recognized it. I felt that he had some moral integrity, but we no longer wore it in Vancouver.

The train service is very good. Thanks to Guo's arrangement, we booked our seats by Tina in advance. The carriage is very clean and spacious. The sofa-shaped leather seats are adjustable, which is equivalent to the first-class seats in high-speed bullet train in China.

As one of the top ten luxury tourist trains in the world, the Canadian is a long-distance tourist train operated by VIA Rail Canada. It has a journey of approximately 4,466 kilometers and a 4-day long. It departs from Vancouver of British Columbia and Toronto of Ontario every week in both directions, runs through the east and west coasts of Canada, passes through four time zones, and almost spans the entire vast land.

The carriage we were in was about 60% occupied. Our destination is Jasper in Alberta. It is really magical of sitting on the sightseeing train with excitement and curiosity, looking at the boundless snow-capped mountains and seeing the long turning front of the train.

Sitting in the observation seats on the second floor of the Skyline (sightseeing) car (with a fully transparent glass roof, it is more convenient for passengers to enjoy the panoramic view of the scenery), we drank fragrant Pu-er tea we brought together, picked it up and put it down, and laughed about the past and present, just like our own lives. Although we didn't buy a sleeper berth, experiencing the coach in Canada took us back to 40 years ago when I was riding the "green train" in China.

As time passed, the passengers in the coach gradually fell

into sleep. The sound of snoring could be heard from time to time, indicating that they enjoyed such a night. At this time, something surprisingly happened. Tap water suddenly came out of the washroom in one end of our coach and flowed onto the carpet in the aisle, affecting nearby guests.

At this time, Mentor Guo took the initiative to inquire, found the conductor, and solved the problem in his fluent English. He also told the mother of the four children on the train to take good care of their children and stop disturbing others in the late night. But instead of appreciation, the mother looked impatient and scolded her children loudly. We all felt a little dissatisfied and a somewhat condemned in our hearts.

Why did the dad come and help? As Mentor Guo said at this time, it is not easy for this mother, she still has a crying baby in her arms, and we should have just be more understanding. At this moment, I was thinking about how important language is in such a foreign land.

After a deep sleep all night, I came to Guo at around 8 o'clock in the morning, and everyone felt more relaxed. After a brief washing, we went to have breakfast, looking forward to arriving at our destination early. As we were in high spirits, the train suddenly stopped. Through the window, we saw the conductors getting off the train and talking nervously, not knowing what was going on. Actually the train had stopped for about 4 hours.

We saw first a minivan, then an ambulance and a police

car came, and for some reason, another ambulance came afterwards. I heard Mentor Guo say that the first ambulance was a testing vehicle and the second one was an emergency ambulance. They were rushing up and down. All the people on site were filled with anxiety. They couldn't help but come to the front and ask Guo what is going on.

He talked about the cause of the incident and explained that the father of that family of six was in a dangerous situation. His breathing was rapid, his pupils were dilated, and his life was in danger. However, he was unable to express his feelings and descript his symptoms clearly in English by himself, which prevented medical and emergency personnel from making effective judgments.

At this moment, no one else can help him in the family express his appeal and explain what happened to him. At the request of the service manager and conductor, Guo came to the ambulance door next to the train and acted as an interpreter and effective communicator for all parts. Thanks to his fluent and accurate expression of medical issues in concise way, the patient called Xu received timely diagnosis and treatment, which alleviated his further critical symptoms. Guo also helped the panic-stricken family of six children and put forward an extremely compromise evacuation suggestion with a compromise plan; he recommended the ambulance personnel in charge of first-aid to pick up the father and the eldest child and go to the local hospital where the temporary stop of train was located for further medical treatment. The remaining three children and their mother were taken to other sleeper carriages for COVID-19 quarantine.

But that's far from the ending. This man and his eldest child were diagnosed with COVID-19 symptoms. If this 'compromise' approach had not been used, the entire train would have been forced to park in the deep mountains and forests due to COVID-19 mishap, or the passengers in the same carriage would have been forced to stop in the mountains due to COVID-19 cases. All passengers will have to be tested, and in more serious cases, they may be quarantined locally. Because we did not protect ourselves and wear masks in all time, thinking about this made our trip full of unexpected events.

Canada is considered as a good life-respecting and people-oriented country with a high level of human rights. In order to save the lives of passengers, medical testing vehicle and emergency ambulance can be mobilized across regions to conduct real-time research and discussions on which hospital to send the patient(s) to for treatment, and how his or her family members should be cared or placed. To this end, Guo stood on cane, walked back and forth in snow between the train staff and the ambulance team. He constantly communicated and coordinated with patients, family members, train personnel and emergency medical staff, and proposed various ways, so that a family evacuation plan can be accepted by the train services and the patient's family.

Later I learned that Guo and his family did not choose to take the COVID-19 vaccines in the entire period epidemic. It is not easy for him to insist on not being infected until now. He is also the only Chinese man on the entire train who can communicate effectively in English. But he rushed forward without thinking anything and helped the suffering family of six solve the problems. Is this the selflessness, enthusiasm and responsibility of his personal nature? We who were there couldn't understand him. Because the Noval Coronavirus infection could occur anytime and anywhere, there is an incubation period, and the four of us have to continue to move forward with the train. Maybe it's with his great love, humanity and kindness! After all, we are all Asians, maybe he feels that he must do this.

After a long period of communication and confrontation between the doctors and patient(s), Guo ran up and down to contact the family members, ambulance men, service manager and patient Xu, the hospital that could treat confirmed COVID-19 only allowed two infected patients to receive treatment, and the other four suspected must be quarantined on the train and cannot accompany the confirmed two as mandatory requested. Because the train stopped suddenly, there were no human living around, it was covered in mist and snow, and there was no public transportation. Even today with the development of the Internet, there is no of any cellular phone signal. The separation of the family of six means losing contact from this moment on.

For this reason, Guo became the 'base' station between the patient Xu and his wife, transmitting messages along the carriages of the train. In the end, the father and son agreed to be taken away by the ambulance and sent to the local hospital. The mother and three small children were transferred by the conductor to a special sleeper cabin for quarantine. All these was also based on Guo's suggestion.

After the train started again, the coach we were was strictly disinfected, and the conductor distributed medical masks to each passenger. Our train finally arrived at the Jasper town station at 17 o'clock, delayed for five hours.

Although preparations for this trip were hasty, Tina Y. Zhang's travel guide was quite detailed. We walked only 5 minutes to the famous Athabasca Hotel, a hotel with a history of 130 years, which is closest to the VIA Rail town station. There are mousse, cow, goat, and deer head specimens hanging in the lobby. Restaurants, bars, and dance clubs around nearby, it exudes the historical flavor of the western cowboys and is full of stories.

After a night's rest, our sightseeing trip officially began. Although it was winter, off-season for tourism, we saw a completely different town of Jasper. It is white and pure. As the sun is shining in the sky, we did not feel cold. It's so warm at noon. This is a famous tourist town that is original, pure, natural, and covered with ice and snow. Every deep breath cleans our heart and lungs, making us extremely relaxing! There are about 5,000 permanent residents here, coming from different countries and regions.

Jasper National Park is one of Canada's famous alpine national parks and the largest around Canadian Rockies. It covers an area of 10,878 square kilometers and is rich in species, dense wild vegetation, and wild animals like red deer, mountain goats, moose, bighorn sheep, black bears, beavers, Rocky Mountain pikas, prairie dogs and caribou roam freely in the mountains and driveways in good numbers.

During our three-day sightseeing adventure, we made appointments with four different taxi drivers to explore and visit the Medicine Lake, Pyramid Lake, Maligne Lake and Maligne Canyon, Athabasca Falls, Fairmont Hotel, etc. Just in winter, mountains, lakes and glaciers complement each other, highlighting the infinite beauty of nature. Especially the last day to go to Marligne Canyon was the most thrilling, almost driving on an icy road. If not for the relaxation and bravery of the indigenous driver Perry, how could we have seen such a wonderful and stunning landscape. I remember an explorer said something after visiting Maligne Lake: "If Lake Louise is a pearl, Lake Maligne is the necklace of pearls." (by William Cornwallis van Horne)

Each taxi driver left a deep and different impression on us. They all have common characteristics, such as: simplicity, enthusiasm, optimism, love for their hometown and kindness to others. What's interesting is that from time to time, advertising slogans are used to introduce the delicacies from various countries here. They hope we can become friends and add their phone numbers to welcome us back. Especially the indigenous man Perry we met on the third day received us. He was humble and introduced us to the local culture and his own inspirational stories along the way.

He was separated from his family when he was a child, was persecuted by white invaders until he was 17 years old, so that he could not speak his own indigenous language and could only speak fluent English. As he turns 50 this year, he chose to lead other tribesmen to fight and litigate with the local ruling government. It is said that he received two state compensation payments in 2022 from the Canadian government. His wife and child were killed in a car accident, he is still alone. He said that we were the only "delegation" from Chinese origin in the past two years.

The next afternoon, out of our surprise, we met Xu and his children again in the hotel lobby, Xu was wearing a white sportswear. It was Mr. Xu who was rescued by us. I was stunned for a moment. Sister Dong said that by some strange coincidence, someone suddenly murmured: "My God". But Guo laughed loudly. We, who were frightened by the strict control of the epidemic, were speechless. Guo said calmly that what happened was that after Mr. Xu was taken away, the hospital doctors arrived in time and his Covid-19 condition was under control. After coordination with the hotel where Xu's wife was staying, the hospital and the hotel taxi gave him the trust without prepayment by a credit card, and then Xu took the Jasper taxi responsible for his transfer when he returned from local hospital. It took more than 5 hours to go back and forth by taxi, and Xu was successfully reunited with his family. The family was later arranged to live upstairs in the hotel. Maybe this was the fate.

Then, at noon on the third day, while we were waiting in the lobby, we unexpectedly met the mother of four children. Is the world so small? Another chance for our encounter? How come you have become our follower and will never leave you! Mentor Guo also said that through his contact and communication again, the couple and their children were finally reunited here, and suggested that they continue to go to the hospital in the Jasper town for examination. It may be due to their ability and language communication problems, but we heard that they were rejected by the Jasper hospital.

In the evening, Mr. Xu said that he had difficulty breathing again and needed emergency treatment. He asked Guo to accompany him there. After we learned about it, we put forward different suggestions. You can communicate by phone, including calling an ambulance, but you cannot go to the hospital, because the follow-up issues are very complicated, how the disease develops, and the responsibilities are huge. We are just passers-by, not his family members. At this critical moment, you can't make any decisions. Moreover, there will also be possible errors in the conversion of English medicines. This is like what people often say: no one knows which comes first, accident or tomorrow.

After a while, Guo said, I wish them safe and success, may God bless them, and I will go back and wait for their news.

On the train back, we met another chatty man. He was a former employee of the Canadian Railways. He had worked on the railway for 34 years and lived in the small downtown of Jasper. According to him, in 1880 the Canadian government needed a large number of cheap labor to build the Pacific Railway. At that time, many young and middle-aged people in coastal areas of China such as Guangdong were treated as "piglets and coolies" by international human traffickers and sold to Canadian gold mines and railway construction companies; after arriving, they were engaged in the most  arduous and dangerous earth and rock engineering operations. It is reported that about 7,000 Chinese labor workers participated in the construction of the entire railway line, and all dangerous and arduous engineering sections were borne by them. After the railway was built, the government at that time did not treat them well, so these labor workers were scattered along the railway and settled down.

Source: RFA mandarin service on 11th June, 2024

《Guo Li, a rights defender of the "poisonous milk powder" incident, suffered multiple obstacles in writing books overseas》

2024.06.11 14:59 ET

Guo Li just completed the book "A Flying Dad" in Canada, detailing the beginning and end of the "poisonous milk powder" incident in China. He said that this is not only a matter of China, but also the whole world, for it is affected by the problem of baby formula and global food safety. (Photographed by reporter Liu Fei)

Guo Li, the parent of a harmed child who was sentenced to five years in prison of Guangdong for defending his rights in the "poisonous milk powder" incident in Beijing and was finally retaliated. During his exile in Canada, he wrote the book "The Taste of Melamine Milk Powder - A Flying Dad". Unexpectedly, he was unreasonably driven away by the landlord in the Van city. He suspected that he was deliberately suppressed by a force behind this and wanted to silence him.

Kidney-stone-Baby's Father Guo Li was denied state compensation in 2022 (1)

Guo Li, the father of a child with poisonous milk powder, was expelled by security guards in Guangzhou 2017 (2)

Guo Li, a victim of China's poisonous milk powder, launched a claim and asked hold the accountability of Mengniu Yashily Dairy enterprise for compensations 2018 (3)

Do you still remember the "poisonous milk powder" incident in China in 2008? It shocked the society in those years. Guo Li, the father of one of the affected children, insisted on defending his rights and demanding compensation from the enterprise that caused the accident, but he was framed by justice and sentenced to five years in prison by the local Guangdong authorities for the crime of "extortion". Later, the Guangdong High Court acquitted him in 2017. He applied for state compensation and was rejected on the grounds that the statute of limitations has passed.

He was tortured in prison, ate moldy rice and ditch water,

and was severely beaten by the jails personal there, resulting in Guo Li's injuries and illness. He chose to leave Beijing when he could not get his proper diagnosis and medical treatment in China.

In an exclusive interview, Guo Li said that he arrived in Van of Canada at the beginning of last year, but did not give up claims and rights defending action, because this is not only his own business, but also the matter of more than 30 million affected families in 2008."It is a goal that should not be given up for all those who pay attention to China's food safety. They have grievances. I hope I can speak it out and say it on their behalf, because on the surface, it's my own business, but it's not like this. Two days ago, I met a person here. He said that his relatives and friends were buying milk powder, infant

Guo's daughter drew a picture and said that Guo was a father flying from the sky or another planet

formula and adult milk powder, and sent it back to China at twice the tagged price." He said that because it (food made from China) was not safe, everyone was afraid of having that. Up to Now, Chinese consumers do not dare to buy it from Hong Kong...Cause there are also plenty of faked brand-name goods

in Hong Kong.

Guo Li drew a picture of himself holding hands with his daughter in a private cell during his five year prison term, conveying the state of missing his daughter. (Photo by Liu Fei)

After being acquitted, he wanted to write a book to record the incident. At first, he contacted some authors, and everyone supported them at the beginning, but then the trouble arose. He recalled sharing the information with a Shandong writer. As soon as the writer was about to write, the other parts was checked secretly by the local security guys. Suddenly, one day, the writer received his community social worker to bring several "strangers" home and said that they heard that you had some contact with Guo Li. You must delete everything in your computer, so in front of them, the writer had to delete all the content of Guo, Li. After that, the writer told me that he couldn't do it anymore.

The picture of Guo, Li, holding hands with his daughter, Guo Li drew
in the single cell of prison (Photo by Liu Fei)

Even writing books in Canada is as blocked as the contact between the families who had been victims in those years. In the past two days, someone called and said that we can't contact you because of your exposure on Chinese milk business scandals. We are so scared, because you have come out of this banned book of China. If you say it publicly, then we will not contact you again. We are fearing and will be very dangerous. Guo Li said that he was kicked out by the PR Chinese landlord last month. Since last year, the landlord has been under constant pressure to let him move out, but according to the " RTB "one-year contract, he has the right to continue to rent for staying.

He said that he paid the rent on time and never made trouble, but the landlord framed him for beating them and false-reported to the police. In the end, the police also said that Guo had the legitimate right to continue to live in the premises, but the landlord still cut off the water, power and lockout of the door, kept him from entering the rental unit, causing him to wander on the street. He said that this was not the behavior of a normal landlord in Canada and he was trying to sue the landlord from the rental or civil issues court. This makes me wonder if I have encountered any force behind them to use the method of 'touching porcelain' or framing （北京话：碰瓷儿）to hope that I will be criminally charged by RCMP police to prevent me from writing this book and defending my rights here in North America.

Guo Li is used to be a well-paid simultaneous interpretation expert in China, and the melamine incident changed his life. The belief of insisting on the struggle put him in Jieyang prison of Guangdong, his wife left him, and his daughter became very alienated from him, but he did not regret. The newly finished book was named "A Flying Dad" because he met his daughter after a full five year sentence in prison.

His daughter drew a picture and said that Guo was a father flying from the sky or another planet. We believe that Guo's daughter will one day understand the significance of him atiding for her and upholding justice for the world.

Reporter: LiuFei Editor: JiaYuan Network Editor: HongWei (Translation: LG)

www.ingramcontent.com/pod-product-compliance
Lightning Source LLC
Chambersburg PA
CBHW060759120626
46557CB00001B/36